KNOWN unto GOD

In Honour of Newfoundland's Missing During the Great War

LIBRARY AND ARCHIVES CANADA CATALOGUING IN PUBLICATION

Gogos, Frank
Known unto God : in honour of Newfoundland's missing during the Great War / Frank Gogos and Morgan Macdonald.

Includes bibliographical references.
ISBN 978-1-55081-322-7

1. World War, 1914-1918--Missing in action--Newfoundland and Labrador--Biography.
2. Soldiers--Newfoundland and Labrador--Biography.
3. Soldiers--Newfoundland and Labrador--Pictorial works.
4. Newfoundland and Labrador--Biography. I. MacDonald, Morgan II. Title.

D639.M56G63 2009 940.4'67718 C2009-906043-4

All images credited at the end, except as noted.
Photos on pages 2, 3 and 6 are of the Newfoundland Memorial Park, Beaumont-Hamel, France, Author's Collection.
Photos on pages 4 and 5 are of a British Commonwealth War Cemetery in France, Author's Collection.
Cover: Homecoming of the Unknown Warrior, Memorial University of Newfoundland and Labrador Archives.

BREAKWATER BOOKS LTD. acknowledges the support of the Canada Council for the Arts which last year invested $20.1 million in writing and publishing throughout Canada. We acknowledge the financial support of the Government of Canada through the Book Publishing Industry Development Program for our publishing activities. We acknowledge the financial support of the Government of Newfoundland and Labrador through the department of Tourism, Culture and Recreation for our publishing activities.

Printed in Canada

Reprinted 2010

Canada Council for the Arts Conseil des Arts du Canada Canada Newfoundland Labrador

KNOWN *unto* GOD

IN HONOUR OF NEWFOUNDLAND'S MISSING DURING THE GREAT WAR

FRANK GOGOS

and

MORGAN MACDONALD

I fancy it's not 'arf my chance
To go on plodding 'neath my pack,
Parading like a snail through France,
My house upon my bloomin' back.

My wants are few, but what I need
Ain't not so much of bully stew,
Nor biscuits, that's a mongrel's feed,
But, matey, just 'twixt me and you –

When winks the early evening star,
And shadows o'er the trenches come –
I wish the sergeants brought a jar,
And issued double tots of rum.

THE TOMMY'S LAMENT
(THE RITZ-LOOS SALIENT)

PATRICK McGILL

THEIR NAME LIVETH
FOR EVERMORE

PREFACE

As the current Commanding Officer of the First Battalion, The Royal Newfoundland Regiment, it is with pride that I express my sincere, heartfelt thanks to Frank and Morgan for the great work they have produced. This book will serve as a companion guide to the memorial plaques that list the names of those men who served in the Newfoundland armed services during the Great War and whose graves are "Known unto God." The plaques, now on two different continents, Beaumont-Hamel, France, and Bowring Park in St. John's, Newfoundland and Labrador, are a medium for reflection for all who bear witness to those names.

These plaques are our "Wall of Reflection." Reflected are names synonymous with all communities in Newfoundland and Labrador. Behind each of these names is a man who once breathed, lived, loved, fought and died for his country. Each and every sailor and soldier in this book has an exceptional story that reflects well upon themselves, their ships, their regiment, and our province. In these pages, their actions are laid out for all to observe. Survivors of the Great War had medals, memories and their lives to live. Those who died in combat may have an appropriate gravesite in the land where they fought. Some soldiers and sailors who died never had a known burial site: such are the circumstances of war. A few families may have been fortunate enough to travel and visit their loved ones with a known grave, but most Newfoundland and Labrador families were never able to visit the graves of their fallen. Worse yet, many families did not know where the final resting places of their fallen were. As time marched on, many families never had closure.

In 1925, the Newfoundland Government paid tribute to those with no known graves by erecting plaques at Beaumont-Hamel. In 2009, our province paid tribute by accomplishing the impossible: we have brought the plaques home. These plaques serve as a sentinel against time. They help provide closure for the descendants of these men. The plaques, and this book, will remind us and future generations of their deeds. I encourage each of you during remembrance week to visit these plaques, or perhaps read this book, to be reminded of their service.

Their graves may be "Known unto God"; however, their names will live on as long as the plaques exist. This book will educate us and future generations as to who these great men were.

F.A. Brennan, Lieutenant-Colonel, Commanding Officer.
First Battalion, The Royal Newfoundland Regiment
1 July 2009

Acknowledgements

This book and its contents are a result of the contributions of many people. The authors would like to extend our sincerest gratitude to all who were involved. We have made every effort to name all contributors. If we have missed your name, we humbly apologize.

We would especially like to thank the people whose contributions, suggestions, and help went above and beyond anything we expected. Special thanks to Cpl. Anthony McAllister who has been most helpful from the first time we met. Chris Butt made his medal collection available to us and also shared his immense knowledge on the subject. Aubrey Halfyard, Chair of the Royal Newfoundland Regiment Museum Committee, made sure we were able to access much material. Gary Browne made a major contribution on behalf of Caroline Ball, as well as sharing his wealth of knowledge. Thanks to: Catherine Tremblay, Veterans Affairs Canada, for giving us prompt access to many of the portraits found in this book; Maude Pinsent, who, right up to the last minute, was ferreting out new pictures and anecdotes to include; Janice Wells for seeing the first stages of the book and making the call to get Breakwater Books interested in this project; Breakwater Books for slotting this book into their busy production schedule on such short notice; Lt. Col. Alex Brennan and RSM Terry Hurley of the Royal Newfoundland Regiment, who gave us tremendous support in our endeavours both with the book and the tablet replication; Avril Williams of the Ocean Villas Tea Room, Auchonvillers, who hosted the replication team in January 2009 and helped inspire us to write this book; Arlene King, Director of the Newfoundland Memorial Park in Beaumont-Hamel, for putting up with us during the cold, wet days of January; the staff of The Rooms Provincial Archives for their help, knowledge, and patience during the research for this book; Michael Martin, who provided much of the material for the Labrador Page; Bert Riggs, Memorial University of Newfoundland Archives; and Neachel Keeping of the City of St. John's Archives.

We would also like to thank the following people who made contributions from their family collections: Myron Arnold, Roy Babstock, Linda Bell, Dan Breen, James F. Cleary, Jack Connors, Oswyn Dawe, Win Desmond, Joe Dobbin, Barney Dooley, Rita Dooley, Wayne Dove, Frank Galgay, Alan Gardner, Ben Gardner, John Kennedy, Bruce King, Kay King, Wilf Miller, Stephen Nulty, John Joseph O'Leary, Ron Penney, Galen and Shirley Gardner Reid, Wayne Slaney, Doug Smith, and Alex Templeton.

And gratitude to our families, who have seen little of us while we worked on these projects. Thank you Loni, Colleen, Wanda, Ferenc, and Mary Kate.

FOREWORD

by Morgan MacDonald

Our hopes are that this book will serve as a companion guide to the three replica memorial tablets located in Bowring Park, St. John's, Newfoundland and Labrador, and to the original tablets in the Newfoundland Memorial Park in Beaumont-Hamel, France. This book is dedicated to the men who served as part of the Newfoundland armed forces during the Great War and is meant to be a brief but informative guide to the names listed on these tablets. It was our wish to highlight all of the numerous stories that occurred during the war and to connect these incredible events to the names on the memorial tablets. However, constraints of time and space dictated that we select just a few. Our goal is to convey to the reader that the names and the history behind these tablets have a greater meaning and story to tell.

Victory Medal

The original three tablets are located in the Newfoundland Memorial Park just outside Beaumont-Hamel as part of a permanent memorial whose creation was overseen by Padre Thomas Nangle in honour of the Newfoundland forces. It is a memorial for those men who served in Newfoundland's national forces on land and sea, who gave their lives, and have no known graves. The replica tablets in Bowring Park were created so that those who may never have the opportunity to visit Newfoundland Memorial Park in France may experience them. We believe that visiting these bronze tablets should not replace the experience of travelling to the site in France, but should educate, and enhance the understanding surrounding Newfoundland's role in the Great War and the remembrance of those who gave their lives for Newfoundland and Labrador.

The information presented here was gathered during our own personal pilgrimage to France. As creators of the replica tablets, we felt it was necessary to impart some of the historic information we had gathered as part of our research. The idea to create replicas of the tablets originated from the Royal Newfoundland Regiment's historic pilgrimage in 2006. Through the financial contributions of the Government of Newfoundland and Labrador and the City of St. John's, we were able to complete the

British War Medal

task of bringing the names of the missing home. Being chosen to complete this historic project has been a tremendously humbling experience and has instilled a strong sense of pride within us. We wanted in some small way to show how proud we are of the Newfoundland forces and to create an enduring tribute to them.

During the Great War our great-grandfather, Corporal Joseph Babstock, fought amongst these men and bore witness to the tragedies and horrors of war. His story lies intertwined with the men whose names are inscribed on these tablets. Joe's story runs parallel to theirs, having been in the same trenches and under the same actions as the men we remember today. One example is that of Captain Ledingham, whose name you can find inscribed on the central Regimental tablet. He was killed at the Battle of Poelcapelle, near Broembeek, Belgium, on October 9, 1917. Ledingham was Joseph Babstock's commanding officer. It is only recently, through this project, that we discovered that a long-time friend throughout my early formative school years was a family member of Captain Ledingham. Look closely and you may find something incredible. Each soldier or seaman represents one of us and we are connected to them more than you may think.

For
Joe

INTRODUCTION

by Frank Gogos

I began a journey with the 821 names memorialized on the three bronze tablets in Beaumont-Hamel in December 2008 when I was asked by Morgan MacDonald to be a part of his team to replicate the bronze tablets and to bring "ours" home. With my journey near completion with the publication of this book, I have had the honour to know many of these men. Not personally, but through their war service records, photographs, and stories from their descendants. I only wish that I could have gotten to know them all. Each name on the tablets represents one of us, our brothers, our husbands, our uncles, our friends, and our fathers. Many Newfoundlanders and Labradorians today have some connection to these tablets from our family past. Our Great-Grandfather Joseph Babstock fought amongst these men, men like Bertram Parsons from Flat Island, Placentia Bay, and James Allan Ledingham of St. John's. He had a cousin, William Babstock of Happy Adventure, who drowned on the trawler HMS *Arfron*. He had many harrowing tales to tell, but kept most stories to himself. Joseph could be counted as one of the "lucky" ones; he survived six battles, countless artillery shells, machine gun fire, trench mortars, bomb assaults, bayonet charges, gas attacks, two wounds, and a year in captivity. Sadly the 592 men listed on the Royal Newfoundland Regiment Tablet did not. Neither did the 114 men listed on the Newfoundland Royal Naval Reserve Tablet nor the 115 men on the Newfoundland Mercantile Marine Tablet.

A good portion of this book is dedicated to the fallen who served with the Royal Newfoundland Regiment. Newfoundland and Labrador's day of sorrow and commemoration is inextricably linked to the Battle of Beaumont-Hamel on July 1, 1916, opening day of the Battle of the Somme. As one commanding officer pointed out in a dispatch on that day, the Newfoundlanders failed only because "... dead men can advance no farther." [1] It is from that moment that the tiny nation had fired into its collective memory sorrow and sadness, a day of reverence to commemorate its own. Beaumont-Hamel became the one singular place of remembrance that overshadowed all others.

However, we must not forget the contribution the Regiment made at Gallipoli, the taking of Caribou Hill, the immense suffering endured during the November Flood, and the rearguard action that saw some of the Regiment the last to leave Cape Helles, or the steely determination to make the "Boches" pay at Gueudecourt on October 12, 1916, for what had happened to the Regiment at Beaumont-Hamel three months earlier. Nor should we forget about the losses sustained at Monchy-le-Preux on April 14, 1917, when yet again the entire Battalion was all but annihilated in an action of questionable planning. And if not for the

Newfoundland military personnel recruiting at Harbour Grace, 1917

fortitude of ten heroic men, nine of whom served with the Newfoundland Regiment, Monchy would have been lost and the British would have suffered incalculable losses trying to recapture the strategic ruins. Regiment men saw action and military success at Ypres, Belgium, on numerous occasions, as well as fighting in the same mud of Passchendaele infamy as the Canadians, and leading the 29th Division over the St. Quentin Canal during the Battle of Cambrai. The accolades the Regiment garnered are impressive, while its losses were sobering. The Regiment was a highly decorated unit within the British Army. It suffered terrible losses. Approximately seventy-five percent of the men who were engaged in active service (those drafted into the 1st Battalion and who saw action in France, Belgium, and Gallipoli) became casualties (wounded or dead), although this number is still up for debate. Approximately twenty-five percent died on active service, never to set foot again on Newfoundland soil. It was one of the highest casualty rates amongst all serving British or Commonwealth units in the Great War.

The tablets at Beaumont-Hamel and the replicas at Bowring Park also commemorate two other Newfoundland forces where the men have no known graves. The Newfoundland Mercantile Marine kept the economic wheels turning, shipping fish overseas and returning with consumables to the island under constant threat of German U-boats. They sailed in all types of vessels, from schooners to steamships; none was safe from the constant threat. The Newfoundland Royal Naval Reserve was a special branch of the British Royal Naval Reserve. They were the first men to sign up and see action, as many were already trained, and participated in the invasion of Gallipoli in early 1915. Some of the men on the Newfoundland Royal Naval Reserve Tablet were killed acting as small-boat boarding parties in the Tenth Squadron Blockade of Germany. As has been said, there was no better race of people suited for the job than the "hardy Newfoundland seaman."

This book was created to put faces to some of the names on those tablets, to tell stories of some of the men, and to help perpetuate their legacy so they won't be forgotten. Families can use this book as a guide for further research. In the final pages of this book all the names on the tablets are listed as they appear on the originals. As much as possible, ages, parents, hometowns, and vessels or battles in which men were lost are listed alongside their names. Short descriptions of the major battles are also here to help the reader better understand the engagements the men participated and died in. A number of sources were used to research these men but the foundation was laid by the Canadian Virtual War Memorial and the Commonwealth War Graves Commission. During the research, changes were made to the records that will not be found on those sites, but these changes come from reliable sources nonetheless.

Many thanks to all those people who made this book happen on such short notice. This book is not meant to be a definitive guide to the men listed on the three tablets, merely a starting point. Remember the sacrifices these men made.

Note to readers: Many of the quotations and excerpts in the following pages contain minor errors in spelling, usage, or punctuation. We have chosen to print the material as it was originally published.

Newfoundland Mercantile Marine

The Mercantile Marine Tablet sits to the right of the Regiment Tablet. One can not overstate the contribution to the war effort by Newfoundland's Mercantile Marine as they plied their schooners, setting a course through U-boat infested waters, crossing the North Atlantic, through the Straits of Gibraltar, and onto destinations within the Mediterranean. Through great risk to themselves, they kept the economic wheels of the tiny nation in motion. They came from all over the island and their success was integral to Newfoundland's ability to support the war effort. Some of these men left port never to be heard from again. The date attributed to the vessel's loss usually refers to the day it left port and was never heard from again.

The Sydney Smith

Not everyone who sailed and was lost on vessels during the war is commemorated on the tablet. The list of names includes only those who were cleared and recorded by customs officials and who were heading for hot zones. Most, if not all, vessels were heading for France, Spain, Portugal, Gibraltar, or destinations within the Mediterranean. Often these schooners carrying salted fish would go to Gibraltar to receive further destination instructions. Dauntless, these vessels braved the North Atlantic, taunting the Germans with names like *Douglas Haig*, or men sailed in old-time barquetines. Even a few larger steamships like the SS *Watagua* fell victim to a U-boat or floundered at sea like the SS *Beverly*. One man, Solomon Clarke, according to a book written by Frank Saunders in 1981, died on the *John Llewelyn* while near St. John's. Captain Dean, the skipper, decided to bring his body ashore, sparing his family a burial at sea. His headstone is in the Old Salvation Army Cemetery in Carbonear alongside his wife Rosalie. The Commonwealth War Graves Commission lists his place of burial in Carbonear, and yet his

name is on the tablets at Beaumont-Hamel. If his body lies beneath the ground, then he would be the sixth man on the memorial to the missing to have a known grave. He was a mate on the schooner *Jorgina* in October 1917 when she aborted her journey to return to Newfoundland to change her crew. The *Jorgina* was lost with all hands when she was torpedoed in March 1918 on her way to Gibraltar. The schooner *Lizzie M. Stanley* was lost in heavy seas east of Cape Race while en route to Catalina from St. Pierre before heading overseas.

Many of the schooners that plied the international waters were manned mostly by family members, as in peacetime. They cleared from places like St. John's, Burgeo, Twillingate, Carbonear, Bay Bulls, and Grand Bank. The steamship *Beverly*, clearing from Harbour Grace, was commanded by Andrew Wilson, Sr., of St. John's, whose son, Andrew Wilson, Jr., also perished on the same vessel along with 22 others.

For their heroism and selfless disregard, they have earned a place of honour for service rendered to King and Country. Without these hardy fishermen and sailors, the main trade of Newfoundland would have ground to a halt and economic devastation would have soon followed.

Mercantile Marine Medal

Richard Owen died on SS Watagua

St. John's Waterfront Finger-pier prior to Great Fire of 1892

The Daily News, June 10, 1918

"No Word of Crew of Torpedoed Schooner"

No word of the crew of the schooner "Cecil Shave" which was reported torpedoed on May 24th, had been received by her owners, A. E. HICKMAN Co. Ltd. Though full enquiries have been made. The schooner left Cadiz for here Feb. 16th last, and word reached her owners May 24th that she had been torpedoed, Hon. Mr. HICKMAN applied to Lloyd's for information of the crew, who in turn enquired from the admiralty. The latter informed the owner that they have no knowledge on the fate of the crew. The schooner carried crew of six all told as follows – Capt. Edgar KEAN, St. John's, formerly of Flower's Island; Scobie McKIE, St. John's, navigator; Charles H. HART, Fogo; John TURPIN, St. John's; Robert HUNT, St. John's and William LEONARD, British Hr., T. B. seamen.[2]

THE SS *BEVERLY*

There is no sadder story on the Newfoundland Mercantile Marine Tablet than that of the disappearance of the 24 crew of the SS *Beverly*.[3] The *Beverly*'s disappearance prompted a marine enquiry. Built by W.E. Woodall & Co. of Baltimore in 1885 as a side-wheel wooden propeller steamboat, and initially named the SS *Baltimore*, the SS *Beverly* worked the Chesapeake Bay until sold to New York interests for passenger inland coastal service between New York and Providence. She lay at a New York dock for two years before Captain Jesse Winter purchased her for the Labrador fishery and sealing trade in 1917. After numerous repairs, refits, and the removal of the top two passenger decks, she was sent to Montreal with cargo, was stranded there, and on her return voyage was stranded again at Riverhead, St. Mary's Bay. The Chief Engineer on this trip, Mr. Dunbar, in his log upon returning to St. John's simply wrote, "Thank God." His duties were then taken over by Patrick Stewart. Afterwards she underwent more extensive repairs and refits at Placentia in an attempt to make her more seaworthy.

W.A. Munn purchased the ship for $125,000 from St. John's shareholders who wished to rid themselves of the troublesome vessel. Munn had also been involved in the cargo shipment to Montreal. The SS *Beverly* was purchased for a trip to Greece with fish and cod oil from his firm in Harbour Grace. Captain A.M. Wilson was

Certificate of Membership in the Society of United Fishermen

THE DAILY NEWS

ar Blaze Near Bowring Park

Last of "Beverley" Goes Up In Smoke

The Newfoundland Historical Society

Wrestling

MONDAY

SINGAPORE PAPER BITTERLY ATTACKS CANAL DIRECTORS

c Notice!

FRUIT ACT

given the official certificate in hopes that, with the shortage of ships caused by the Great War, the vessel could be sold at profit to French or Greek interests.

On the Saturday before departure three firemen from the St. John's area returned to the city by train after being denied shore leave. They went to see their families for one last time. Angry, Munn cabled St. John's and asked that the three men, Thomas Carrigan of Logy Bay, John Power of Outer Cove, and John Noftall of St. John's, be arrested and returned to Harbour Grace to catch the Monday departure of the SS *Beverly*. Constable Edward Whelan, who escorted the three men back to Harbour Grace, said at the enquiry the men told him the "... ship was leaking heavily. They said they never expected to reach home again owing to the condition. She shook so much when the engine was working ..."[4] The firemen said the only reason they were going was because of the high wages being paid out. Noftall said to Whelan, as the train came past the heavily laden SS *Beverly* moored at Riverhead, "She is going to be our coffin, boys."[5]

Loaded with 11,000 quintals of fish and 50 barrels of cod liver oil, she left Harbour Grace on a stormy Monday evening, January 21, 1918, and was never heard from again. The contents were insured for $400,000 against storm or war loss, and Munn expected to fetch up to $300,000 for the sale of the vessel once the cargo was delivered to Greece. At 33 years old, she was on her first transatlantic voyage. The ensuing enquiry found that she was not suited for such a voyage, especially in the dead of winter, and was never intended for such work by her builders. By clearing off the two decks they had exposed the engine room to rogue waves if the wheelhouse was washed away, not an uncommon thing to happen to schooners crossing the Atlantic. The hull was lightly built from a foot or so from the waterline and not able to withstand winter seas in the mid-Atlantic. The enquiry also found the Newfoundland Government ship surveyor, also a Lloyd's insurance agent, erred grievously when he okayed the vessel for such work. He also accepted $200 in gifts from W. A. Munn, which the enquiry said should have led to an immediate dismissal. However, the Newfoundland Government had no means to prevent a vessel from leaving port if deemed unseaworthy, something that changed after the final report of the Marine Enquiry was released.

The last remnants of the SS *Beverly* went up in flames on Regatta Day 1933. Mr. Duff, owner of the York Theatre, had purchased and removed the passenger decks from the *Beverly* with the intention of opening a tea room or dance hall in the vicinity of the newly opened Bowring Park. Placed on Molloy's Lane, the passenger decks were rebuilt to look like a riverboat on land. At the time of the fire, the decks had been abandoned and were in a state of disrepair. The structure was last used for summer apartments. The well-built structure burnt to the ground, the intensity of the fire giving the folks at the nearby Sanatorium a troublesome night.

WAR AND ENLISTMENT, 1914

Field Marshall Kitchener,
Secretary of State for War U.K.

The spark that ignited the First World War came with the assassination of Archduke Ferdinand, heir to the Austro-Hungarian throne, in Sarajevo, on June 28, 1914. Europe at this time was rife with imperial rivalry that spread across the globe, competed in arms races, and formed diplomatic alliances among the various European powerhouses; the assassination provided a pretext to mobilize large armies throughout Europe. It was the match that lit the powder keg. The Allies – Russia, France, British Empire (including Canada, Australia, New Zealand, India, South Africa, and Newfoundland), Italy, Japan, Portugal, and later, the United States – faced off with the Central Powers – Germany, Austro-Hungary, Bulgaria, and the Ottoman Empire. The Russians moved west towards Germany with the knowledge that France would join and occupy Germany on her western border. Austro-Hungary moved her armies towards Serbia in the south and Russia in the east. Germany split her armies, one to occupy the Russians, the other to advance through Belgium and into northern France. Once Germany crossed into Belgian territory, the British were obliged by treaty to declare war on Germany. The treaty, to which Britain was a signatory, guaranteed Belgium neutrality. Britain's declaration of war came on August 4 and dragged Canada, Australia, New Zealand, South Africa, India, and Newfoundland into the fray.

Newfoundland responded quickly. She first committed the trained Newfoundland Royal Naval Reservists, raised their number to 1000, and then undertook to raise a regiment to fight on land. Later Newfoundland would also contribute a forestry battalion. Newfoundland had no standing military force at the outbreak of the war. There were various militias and paramilitary groups affiliated with religious organizations such as the Anglican Church Lads' Brigade (CLB), the Roman Catholic Cadet Corps, the

Methodist Guards, and the Presbyterian-sponsored Highlanders. Another group, with no religious affiliation, the Legion of Frontiersmen, existed in St. John's and St. Anthony. When the recruiting office at the CLB Armoury opened its doors on Harvey Road, it was the cadets from these city groups that made up a good portion of the "First Five Hundred" or "Blue Puttees" as they came to be known. It was a colourful bunch of recruits that assembled on the Pleasantville grounds on the north shore of Quidi Vidi Lake in September 1914, many of them sporting the various garb that made up their cadet uniforms. Later, standard uniforms were supplied, but the lack of khaki material forced them to use blue leg wraps, or puttees, earning them the title "Blue Puttees." Later in the war, to be a "Blue Puttee" was a badge of honour amongst the troops and the Newfoundland people.

Group photo of Newfoundland officers, September 1914

Issuing of arms in Britain

While Newfoundland set about building a regiment, the war in Europe was heating up. The small professional British Army was engaged in a fighting retreat with the Germans in Belgium and was all but wiped out. The French threw everything at the German steamroller, losing 200,000 men in seven days. By October, both nations, though badly mauled, managed to slow the German advance, initiating outflanking manoeuvres that led to the formation of defensive entrenchments along a 400-mile stretch from the coast of Belgium, through northern France, to the borders of Switzerland. This line, which would remain practically unchanged for the duration of the war, provided the killing grounds that swallowed up millions of men in a terrible war of attrition.

The First Five Hundred, or Blue Puttees, embarked for England aboard the SS *Florizel* on October 4, 1914. The day before, with their ill-fitting uniforms hidden underneath greatcoats, lacking military headdress and firearms, this rag-tag unit had marched through the streets of St. John's, with cheering throngs of supporters lining the parade route. Newfoundland was embarking upon the world stage and was beaming with pride.

2nd Contingent, C and D Companies, aboard the* Stephano, *March 1914.

First Five Hundred on board the SS* Florizel, *at anchor in St. John's, October 4, 1914

Once in England they settled down into a training regime that would turn these men into efficient fighting units. They fought hard to keep their identity as Newfoundlanders even when pressured to be made a part of the Canadian Contingent. "We are all very particular here that we should not be classed as Canadians … we are much prouder of our distinction as Newfoundlanders …"[6] Eventually the patriotic Newfoundlanders won out, kept their identity, and were moved to Scotland to further their training throughout the rest of 1914 and the first half of 1915.

Meanwhile, Britain and France opened up a third front on the Gallipoli Peninsula in Turkey in April 1915. The first Newfoundlanders to see action were members of the Newfoundland Royal Naval Reserve who were stationed on the HMS *Cornwallis* when the invasion of Turkey began. Strategists assumed the Ottoman Empire's fighting forces were in shambles: either an easy victory over the Turks would ensue and Britain could free Russia's Black Sea Naval Fleet, or Germany would be forced to prop up Turkish defences, thereby weakening her manpower on the Western Front. It would be an engagement that would lead to Allied embarrassment, but not before the Newfoundland Regiment would play its part in Gallipoli.

2nd Contingent of the Newfoundland Regiment marching in St. John's before shipping out overseas, 1915

GALLIPOLI

Soldiers shaving in trenches

In September 1915 a regiment stepped onto Kangaroo Beach in Suvla Bay, marking the first time in almost a hundred years, since the War of 1812, that a regiment raised in Newfoundland became involved in a war. Gallipoli Peninsula is in the eastern Mediterranean and was a part of the Ottoman Empire (Turkey). Allies Britain and France opened this front to gain access to the Russian Black Sea Fleet, to put more pressure on Germany, and were aided by British dominions Australia, New Zealand, and Newfoundland.

The 1st Battalion, Newfoundland Regiment embarked on the great adventure. These hardy fishermen, store clerks, sons of prominent merchants, lumbermen, and townie corner boys swaggered off the transport lighter in the darkness of the Turkish night. They had come to relieve the battered Royal Scots and take their place in the "incomparable" 29th Division, the only volunteer-raised regiment amongst eleven pre-war veteran battalions. On the morning of the first day, the Regiment had its first casualties. Within three days the Regiment would record its first two deaths. Within a week the entire Battalion was manning a trench on the front line.

The Newfoundland Regiment never fought any major engagements in Gallipoli, but their contributions and their sacrifices were real. From the outset the biggest obstacle the Regiment and others on the Peninsula faced was sickness brought on by the heat and flies. Dysentery, enteritis, and jaundice were demons to which many succumbed. The Newfoundlanders were a sturdy stock that stood well, but sickness ravaged them nonetheless. Some soldiers took sick in Gallipoli and eventually found themselves medically discharged, while others died on hospital ships based offshore and were buried at sea.

It was a weakened Battalion that won its first decorations for valour in the field. Early in November, the Newfoundlanders, tired of being sniped at by the

The Cornwallis *evacuating Gallipoli: "Naval Guns Firing at Shore"*

1914-1915 Star awarded for active service in the field before December 31, 1915

Turks at night from a hill located halfway in no man's land, decided to put a stop to it. A small band of Newfoundlanders approached Caribou Hill in the day, knowing the Turks would come out at night to occupy the position. After nightfall three Turks approached Caribou Hill (as it became known later). Lt. Donnelly and six others challenged them and a brief firefight ensued, leaving two Turks dead and one Newfoundlander slightly wounded. The wounded Newfoundlander was sent back to get reinforcements for an anticipated Turkish attack. Eight men answered the call and headed out to the hill in the darkness. They came across a party of Turks trying to encircle Donnelly's post. The Newfoundlanders drove the Turks back and five of the eight became casualties, one fatally. Because of their actions, no more trouble came from this hill for the rest of the Gallipoli campaign.

November saw many storms; the most severe struck Suvla Bay on the 26th. A four-hour thunderstorm, the intensity of which most Newfoundlanders had not experienced before, filled the trenches with water. Eventually the build-up of water broke through the trenches on the higher slopes, and rivers of mud and debris came sweeping through the Newfoundland position from both flanks. Many of the men were lucky to escape drowning. The next day, cold, dejected, and tired, they worked as best they could to repair the damage left behind. The weather then changed to an icy hurricane with sleet, followed by snow. By the next morning the water in the trenches was coated with half an inch of ice. More than 200 of the Allied Forces either drowned or froze to death. Scores more were wounded, including 150 from the Newfoundland Regiment, but thankfully none of the wounds was fatal.

Cape Helles, Gallipoli

Before the November storms, the decision to abandon the Gallipoli Peninsula had been already put into motion. The first order of evacuation was from Suvla Bay. By December 19 the last of the Newfoundlanders boarded a lighter for the island of Mudros. Their rest at Mudros was short-lived, and they embarked for Cape Helles on the tip of the Gallipoli Peninsula on December 22. The Battalion took over the work duties of the Greek Labour Corps, building piers and quarrying rock, making it appear that everything was normal. On January 9, 1916, the last remnants of the British evacuated Gallipoli for good as Lt. Owen Steele of the Newfoundland Regiment and a few men stepped onto a lighter, bidding farewell as timed explosives lit up the abandoned ammunition dumps, illuminating the Turkish night and raining debris all around them, breaking one man's arm in three places.

Seven men who died on hospital ships offshore of Gallipoli were buried at sea and are commemorated on the tablets at Beaumont-Hamel.

Those heroes that shed their blood and lost their lives … you are now lying in the soil of a friendly country. Therefore rest in peace. There is no difference between the Johnnies and the Mehmets where they lie side by side here in this country of ours … You the mothers who sent their sons from far away countries, wipe away your tears. Your sons are now lying in our bosom and are in peace Having lost their lives on this land they have become our sons as well.

–Atatürk (leader of the turkish people)[7]

D Company, First Newfoundland Regiment, marching at Pleasantville, St. John's, 1915

Beaumont-Hamel: Trench Raids

Michael Francis Kennedy

William Robert McNiven

Fifty-seven handpicked men of all ranks underwent three weeks of intensive training prior to July 1, 1916, to be used for a trench raid in an effort to capture German prisoners before the launch of the "Greatest Battle" of all time. Led by the Battalion Intelligence Officer, Captain Bertram Butler, and conditioned by the aptly named Lt. Charlie Strong, these men of the Newfoundland Regiment prepared to infiltrate the German positions at night. They trained, ate, and slept together and were segregated from their Regiment. By the end of training they became experts in the use of bomb, bayonet, and revolver in close quarters combat.

The first of two raids commenced during the night of June 26 in conjunction with the 29th Division Artillery. The Artillery bombarded sections of the intended target and then moved the bombardment for half an hour to allow the raiding party to get into a German communication trench that ran into the northern arm of the Y-Ravine. The Artillery commenced bombardment on that section of trench at 1 a.m. Their objective was to capture German prisoners and gather intelligence on the German defensive preparedness. With their faces blackened and all identifications stripped from their uniform and person, armed with "revolvers, rifles, bayonets, knob-berries, knives, and mills bombs" and carrying two twenty-foot-long Bangalore torpedoes to blast the wire in front of the German trenches, the 57 Newfoundlanders set off into the night. The first torpedo failed to open up the wire completely and the second one was deployed but failed to explode. Wire cutters were being used when the men were exposed by enemy flares. Rifle fire erupted and a reluctant Butler, having lost the element of surprise, ordered the men to withdraw.

The next night the raiding party was asked to make another attempt. Captain Butler's reconnaissance revealed gaps already in the wire. He laid low in a shell-hole with Private John Lukins while he waited for the main party to join him in no man's land. The raiders came within 20 yards of the German trenches when a flare went up and exposed their positions. A fire fight ensued and the Newfoundlanders inflicted heavy casualties on the crowded German trench with rifle and bombs. Some of the raiders got caught up in the wire, some managed to get into the trench, two were severely wounded and taken prisoner. One of them survived. A third man jumped into the trench: Private George Phillips bayoneted several Germans before retiring to a shell-hole, using all his ammunition before retreating to his own front line in the morning. For his actions he received the Military Medal and the Russian Order of St. George.

George Phillips, M.M. & Russian Order of St. George

Phillips would join the annals of the missing at Gueudecourt four months later. John J. Cahill, mentioned in dispatches, died of wounds in enemy hands on July 5. Pte. Lukins was shot through the neck and died, remaining in no man's land. Altogether six men were killed and thirteen wounded. Butler and his men spent a good portion of the night retrieving the wounded at great risk to themselves. Although they failed to capture any Germans they did come back with the knowledge that the week-long artillery bombardment had little effect on the numbers and preparedness of the enemy. Pte. Lukins had a brother who would die three days later and is buried inside the park in the Hawthorn Ridge No. 2 Cemetery.

George Phillips Citation

"For Gallantry in the raid on the night of 28/29 June, 1916." 88th Brigade Lists.

"Displayed conspicuous gallantry in the raid 27/28 June south of Beaumont-Hamel. He entered the enemy's trench and accounted for several of the enemy single handed. After getting out of the trench he went back again to try and obtain some identification. Remained out all night, and had to cut his way back through enemy's wire. This man also took part in the attack south of Beaumont-Hamel on July 1st and showed great gallantry. He was wounded on this date."[8]

ANCRE

BEAUMONT-HAMEL

Francis Galgay

John Breen

Norman Coultas

George & John "Jack" Lukins

FRANCE,
AUGUST 26th-1916.

DEAR MISS BUCKLEY,-

I have been handed a letter addressed by you to CAPTAIN O'BRIEN asking for particulars re Jack Lukins.

Well Miss Buckley he certainly was a fine chap, fearless and cool. I guess you have heard of the raid made on the German trenches on June 28th., Jack was my leading man, and we got on the German parapet together. It was a rather dark night, and we reached this point apparently unseen, and we waited for our main party to arrive. Our main party did not get quite up to us when the row started, and we started a little scrap on our own account. We were lying together in a little depression, and as he had a rifle he was blasing away for all he was worth and certainly did some damage. I was rather busy also, but during a lull I noticed that he wasn't firing. I heard him say, " Sir I'm finished" and about that time I got hit myself. When I cam too I investigated, and found that the poor chap was about finished. As far as know he did not speak after I heard him say the preceding words. He was hit through the lower part of the neck, and he undoubtedly saved my life. Whoever fired the shot certainly paid for it, as I dropped a bomb right in the place where it came from.

I thought to have got into the German trench, but when Jack got hit I had to give it up. He was certainly a brave man, and to him was largely due the success of my raid. I shall never forget him, as he was the bravest chap I ever met.

Please convey to his wife my deepest sympathy in her loss of such a fine chap.

War is an awful game. It was his turn that night, others July 1st., and perhaps mine to-morrow. Of course we have the thing before us every day, and are getting used to it. We all hope to come through alright, but one never knows when he is in for it.

Again expressing my deepest sympathy, and my warmest appreciation of a brave comrade, I am,

Yours very truly,

SGD, BERT BUTLER.[9]

Beaumont-Hamel: Battle

July 1st, 1916

Hardly a family was left untouched by the tragedy that befell the Newfoundland Regiment on this day. Of the approximately 801 men who went over the top, only 68 answered the roll call the next morning. It was the first day of the Battle of the Somme, one of the largest offensives ever launched in the history of warfare. So sure were the British in its success, the top commanders threw caution to the wind, and by the end of the day there were nearly 20,000 British soldiers lying dead over a twelve-mile front. Another 38,000 wounded soldiers clogged the firing line as well as various communications and support trenches, field hospitals, and cellars all over the Somme. The Newfoundland Regiment's role was especially tragic amongst a day of calamity. They were not called upon to attack in the first or second waves, but on the third.

The British attacked at 7:30 in the morning, preceded by many days of artillery bombardments and ten minutes after a mine exploded at Hawthorn Ridge on the Newfoundlanders' left. Unable to attack from the firing line, they were forced to leave their support trench in the rear one hour and forty-five minutes after the initial charge, largely because of the mass of dead and dying choking up the trench system from the first two waves. With their chins tucked into their chests as if they were walking through a snowstorm, they advanced from far behind the British front line. Silhouetted against the skyline, the Newfoundlanders were the only ones advancing towards the Germans in that sector. The Essex Regiment failed to advance with them in support. Some fell before reaching the British front line; others got caught in the uncut wire; a select few fell just short of the German front line in front of the Y-Ravine; while the majority fell in a crossfire of machine gun bullets in no man's land. Most of the men congregated in two areas where there were openings in the wire. The most striking feature of no man's land was a lone stripped and battle-charred tree where the bodies piled high. Today that solitary tree is revered as the Danger Tree. On this day many of Newfoundland's bravest sons lay strewn all over the battlefield as did the nation's future.

ON THIS DAY NEWFOUNDLAND'S BRAVE SONS LAY STREWN ALL OVER THE BATTLEFIELD AS DID THE NATION'S FUTURE.

Newfoundland soldiers in a support trench

There were many tales of heroism and sorrow, suffering and pain. But to the country who asked these brave men to fight, it was devastating. It was the first real battle for their proud Regiment. As news began trickling back home, people gathered around cable stations and post offices, waiting for days to find out if their loved ones had survived. The battle went so badly that as many as 115 men had completely disappeared. The Newfoundland Government spent months trying to find them on POW lists coming from the Red Cross. But they lay still in no man's land in front of one the strongest German positions along the Somme battlefield. There were no prisoners taken July 1. Letters were sent to the families months later stating that the Newfoundland Government no longer believed the men were prisoners of war, that they were missing in action and presumed killed. When Beaumont-Hamel finally fell in November 1916, British soldiers began burying their dead, and many of the men they interred at that time were the bones of Newfoundland's gallant sons. To this day many of the missing still lie just underneath the surface in the Newfoundland Memorial Park.

AUCHONVILLERS

Newfoundland's losses were staggering. Not one officer who went over the top that morning escaped unscathed. Four members of the Ayre family were lost. Gerald Walter Ayre is remembered on the Beaumont-Hamel tablet. Many of the wounded were left for long periods of time on the battlefield. Some died and were never found; 290 men of the Regiment were killed on July 1 (and raids prior to) or later died of wounds. Almost half (143) were never identified and today are commemorated on the bronze tablets at the base of the Caribou Monument. Five men were later identified and were interred in nearby cemeteries. There are many Commonwealth War Graves Cemeteries in the area and a Caribou headstone can be found in most.

BEAUMONT-HAMEL: QUOTES

George Sparks

"Two of the bravest men in the Newfoundland Regiment, in my opinion, were Lieut. Roy Ferguson and Sergt. Ollerhead. When I was lying down on the morning after the advance had been held up and there was not another soul advancing, Lieut. Ferguson went towards the German trench with his revolver grasped in his outstretched right hand … Sergt. Ollerhead … advanced to see what had become of his officer. In my humble opinion these two men advanced towards the German trench knowing that certain death must be the inevitable result."

- Unnamed source, an eyewitness officer wounded in no man's land[10]

"It was a magnificent exhibition of disciplined courage."

- Lt. Gen. Sir Hunter-Weston[11]

"It was a magnificent display of trained and disciplined valour, and its assault only failed of success because dead men can advance no farther."

- General De Lisle, 29th Division Commander[12]

Robert Porter

"Nothing could be finer than the manner in which the Regiment steadily advanced in the face of appalling fire, which simply swept the men away."

"… and to assure them … the families in mourning … that nothing could have been finer than the gallant manner in which they met their death."

"Attack Strength July 1:809, all ranks - (8 more than most reports.)"

"In addition there are 89 men, all ranks, in reserve who did not go over the top."

- Report from Lt. Col. Hadow, Commanding Officer 1st Newfoundland Regiment[13]

From the wounded soldiers: "Is the Colonel pleased?"[14]

Robert Bruce Reid

Howard Morry was a part of the ten percent reserve kept back at Beaumont-Hamel who witnessed the battle and its aftermath.

"FRONT LINE LIKE A BUTCHER SHOP IN HELL."[16]

Referring to the two gaps which most of the men tried to pass through:

"89 died at one gap and 82 out at the other ... It was an awful sight for us survivors to see, our good friends and buddies for years, piled up like that."[15]

Days after the battle Morry remembers:

"... We went in and took over our old lines again, and our first job was to finish burying our dead. Some job it was too, take these black and swollen bodies, taking the equipment off them. When the equipment belt is open, what a gush of air out of the swollen bodies. Then we had to take their paybooks, letters, watches etc, mark them and turn them in so that they could be sent to their relatives. We just dug a hole alongside the body and rolled them in with a little simple prayer. It is a grand thing that mothers could not see the way that their sons died."[17]

William Ryan

Joseph Hollahan

Leonard Barrett

"IT'S QUITE LONESOME HERE NOW, ALL ME CHUMS ARE GONE ... I DON'T MUCH CARE. I AM SATISFIED TO DIE FOR MY KING AND COUNTRY."[18] Victor Carew survived the horrors of Beaumont-Hamel but would lose his life at Masnieres on November 20, 1917, and is memorialized on the tablets at Beaumont-Hamel.

HAWTHORNE #2

Dear Madam
Mrs K Morrissey
44 Wickford Street

For some time past the Imperial Government have been making enquiries in relation to those men of the First Newfoundland Regiment who have been reported missing since the action of 1st July. I very much regret to state, however, that from the correspondence which has taken place, a copy of which I enclose, it is evident that none of them are Prisoners of War in Germany, and the authorities are, therefore, reluctantly forced to the conclusion that all these gallant men, whose names are given in the enclosed list, and one of whom was very dear to you, were killed in that fateful action on the 1st of July.

I desire to express to you on behalf of the Government, as well as myself, the sincerest sympathy in this time of sorrow. We feel the loss of our loved ones, but it will, no doubt, be some consolation to you to think that he, for whom you now mourn, willingly answered the call of King and Country, did his part nobly, and fell, facing the foe, in defence of the principles of Righteousness, Truth and Liberty. Though he has laid down the earthly weapons of warfare, he now wears the Soldier's Crown of Victory, and his name will be inscribed upon the Glorious Roll of Honor, and be held in fragrant memory by all his country-countrymen. When the victory is won, and Peace again reigns upon the earth, it will be a comforting thought to you that in this glorious achievement he bore no small part.

I trust that you may have the Grace and consolation of the Great Father of us all at this time.

With sincere sympathy
Believe me to be
Your obedient Servant
Colonial Secretary[19]

Bernard Cleary

John Roy Ferguson

The following letter was written by Patrick Connors, father of James Patrick Connors, on September 8, 1920. By this time Patrick, his wife, and family had moved from Newfoundland and were living in New Glascow, Nova Scotia.

In answer to your letter, I can't give you any information concerning my dear sons death, James P Connors, No 209, 1st Newfoundland Regiment, he was one of the Blue Puttee Boys. The only information that I can give you is that he was missing July 1st, 1916. I can't give you any account of his grave or where he was buried. As far as I know his bones may be blackening today, on some part of No Mans Land. I got but very little satisfaction concerning his death or I never even got anything belonging to him and as far as decorations are concerned we didn't even get only the medal for 1914 & 1915. His age is 23, the son of Patrick & Mary Ann Connors. His birth place is West End St John's, any other information I cannot give you. I am waiting every day for further information from you concerning him. If I knew anything about him I would only be too glad to have the papers filled out and sent to you.[20]

" AS FAR AS I KNOW, HIS BONES MAY BE BLACKENING TODAY, ON SOME PART OF NO MAN'S LAND. "

OCTOBER 12TH, 1916

GUEUDECOURT

Clarence Bastow

The Regiment left the Somme for a period of rebuilding after the near annihilation at Beaumont-Hamel. After ten weeks in Flanders, the Newfoundlanders left Belgium on October 8, 1916, to rejoin the fray on the Somme. On short notice and with no preparatory training, the men entered the firing line on the night of October 11, unsure if they were there in a defensive or offensive manoeuvre. For this action they were attached temporarily to the 12th Division and faced a fresh enemy division, the 6th Brandenburg, a determined enemy known unofficially as the "Iron Division." The men were eager to get back into action after spending the previous ten weeks around Ypres digging trenches, laying barbed wire, and other various fatigues.

LONDON

Joseph Babstock & Bertram Parsons

The Regiment began to suffer heavy casualties from intensive shelling on October 11, and by noon the next day, the number of casualties had already reached 104, two hours before the scheduled attack. The objective of the Newfoundlanders was to take Hilt Trench and then establish a new line in front of the captured trench. With the aid of a creeping barrage, a newly devised tactic that would allow the infantry to advance behind a curtain of artillery fire, the Regiment would attack. The creeping barrage would also lead to many casualties amongst the Newfoundlanders either from following the barrage too closely or from premature bursts from shrapnel shells. The creeping barrage was effective in keeping the Germans' heads down and rendering their machine gun units ineffective, for when the barrage lifted, the Newfoundlanders were right there in the trench. With bomb and bayonet and with their fallen comrades at Beaumont-Hamel on their minds, the intrepid Newfoundlanders resolutely took and held their portion of Hilt Trench. An attempt by Lt. Cecil Clift to lead two platoons forward 100 yards in front of the newly won Hilt Trench to build another line failed and led to the platoons being wiped out.

Hardy Frederick Snow

On their left the Essex Regiment, who were increasingly coming under heavy fire from an exposed left flank of their own, withdrew at about 4 p.m. from Hilt Trench to the original starting line, exposing Newfoundland's left flank. Undaunted, Captain March thinned out the Newfoundlanders to occupy the 1st Essex abandoned portion of Hilt Trench. With bombing parties, the Battalion secured the trench and put up a block to prevent the Germans from attacking using the adjoining Bayonet Trench, which was still under German command. Within the hour, the Germans formed a counterattack group that was repulsed by the thinned out Newfoundland Regiment with aid from their Lewis Gunners. They were not relieved from the newly won trench until 3 a.m. on October 13.

Cecil B. Clift

Chesley Gough

Gueudecourt became a Newfoundland success where Beaumont-Hamel was a tragedy. It was one of the few successes in the Battle of Le Transloy. Brigadier-General Cayley wrote, "The success was the more gratifying as it was the only real success recorded that day."[21] The Regiment captured their first trophies of war and won praise from captured Germans of the Iron Division for their "élan" or "esprit des corps." They acquitted themselves heroically and showed everyone they could not only die well, but fight too. Richard Neville, Alfred Manuel, and Bernard Carroll all won Military Medals at Gueudecourt only to be added to the annals of the missing at Monchy-le-Preux. Cyril Gardner of British Harbour won his Distinguished Conduct Medal while leading two other men in a surprise attack on a German party, taking prisoners. He would later add a Bar to this award for his part in single-handedly capturing 72 Germans while unarmed in action at Sailly-Saillisel several months later. He too would disappear at Monchy-le-Preux. From October 10-13 the Regiment suffered 239 casualties; 49 men would later be added to the names of the missing with no known graves at Beaumont-Hamel. An estimated 250 Germans were killed by the Newfoundlanders in their part of the battle.

Louis Brown

Robert Butler

SAILLY-SAILLISEL

In late January and early March 1917 the Newfoundland Regiment was embroiled in side actions around the destroyed village of Sailly-Saillisel. Often forgotten by historians, as the Battle of the Somme officially ended in November 1916, the Newfoundlanders added more medals and distinctions while supporting other brigades. A number of men on the Regiment Tablet were added from the actions that took place near or inside the ruined village.

On January 27, 1917, the Newfoundland Regiment were in support of an attack launched by the 87th Brigade. They provided machine gun and trench mortar support as well as stretcher duty to bring in wounded soldiers. Some of the men eager to join the fight went over the top of their own volition. Company Sergeant Major Cyril Gardner of British Harbour was in no man's land after the attack, supposedly keeping an eye on his own men, when he stumbled across a company of the enemy in a trench that had been by-passed by the advancing 87th Brigade. Acting quickly, he seized a gun (as he was unarmed) and said to a German officer, "*Tres bon.* You're late. Everyone else had *Kameraded.*"[22]

Surprisingly, 72 Germans capitulated to Gardner. Triumphantly, Gardner marched his prize back to his own line, but not without incident. As he approached, a British officer confronted him and his prisoners, threatening to shoot them. If not for Gardner's coolness and his brevity in stopping the British officer, it is possible that these Germans would have been slaughtered. In recognition of his actions, a decorated officer pinned Germany's highest military medal, the Iron Cross First Class, onto Gardner's breast. Later, the British would add a Bar to the Distinguished Conduct Medal he had won at Gueudecourt. Lt. Bert Holloway received a mention in Field Marshall Haig's April 9th dispatch for his role in an unofficial reconnaissance that took him up to a mile behind enemy lines and led to the capture of six more Germans. Both men would lose their lives and join the missing at Monchy-le-Preux.

Cyril Gardner

The Iron Cross First Class given to Cyril Gardner by a German officer

The Regiment returned to the area in late February and were mired in the mud of the thawing winter battleground. During the days of March 1-3, the Newfoundlanders were again placed in support of a minor action led by the 86th Brigade. This time the Germans launched counterattack after counterattack, determined not to give more ground to the British. Using bombs and Lewis Guns, the Newfoundlanders held their positions in the trench despite the resolution of the enemy to gain ground. After Sailly-Saillisel the Newfoundlanders were moved north in preparation for their involvement at the Battle of Arras. Sixteen men joined the ranks "Known Unto God" from the actions at Sailly-Saillisel.

"… AFTER HE HAD TAKEN THE PRISONERS HE PICKED UP A REVOLVER OFF A DEAD MAN."

–COLONEL HADOW, APRIL 6, 1917[23]

GUARDS

THERE ARE 16 MEN ON THE REGIMENT TABLET WHO HAVE NO KNOWN GRAVES FROM THE ACTIONS THAT TOOK PLACE AT SAILLY-SAILLISEL.

Garland Powell

Bert Holloway

APRIL 14TH, 1917

MONCHY-LE-PREUX

Joshua Tucker

Monchy-le-Preux is a sleepy French village just east of Arras. The village is situated on top of a hill rising out of the low lying countryside. It was a major German stronghold and one of the key objectives of the Battle of Arras, launched on April 9, 1917. It fell into British hands on the 11th. On the night of the 13th the Newfoundlanders moved forward alongside the Essex Regiment to take up positions on the firing line. Monchy-le-Preux was a pronounced salient. The *War Diary* stated: "The result of this operation if successful would be a position balloon shaped blown from Monchy-le-Preux which was already the apex of a salient."[24] On the morning of April 14, the Essex and Newfoundland Regiments, with approximately 1400 men between them, were ordered to attack along the entire eastern edge of Monchy and move eastward to Infantry Hill, some 1000 yards ahead along an ever-widening arc 1200 yards wide, penetrate, and dig into two sizable woods located 500 yards northeast and southeast of the hill, with no support on either flank and with no support coming up from the rear.

The main purpose of the attack was to capture Infantry Hill, "securing the observation platform" that made Monchy-le-Preux's position precarious and valuable depending on who controlled the hill. To fully utilize the Monchy gain on April 11, Infantry Hill had to be taken. The planning of the attack, however, was questionable. Considering the importance of Monchy-le-Preux to the overall objective of the Battle of Arras, it should never have been risked. The Newfoundlanders found the first lines of German defence lightly manned, and "C" and "D" Companies advanced up to the hill and started down the other side, facing stiff opposition. "A" Company advanced on the right towards Machine Gun Wood, and "B" Company was assigned to mop-up duty.

William Norman

Edmund Dunphy

Richard Neville

Reports from the Essex Regiment coming back spoke of Germans in great numbers gathered in the woods past the hill. The ensuing German counterattack killed and captured hundreds of the Newfoundland and Essex soldiers. Whole platoons disappeared. Newfoundland's losses at Monchy were appalling. Of the 611 men from the Newfoundland Regiment who attacked, there were a total of 488 casualties according to the official *War Diary*, which may also include the later action of Les Fosses Farm: a casualty rate of eighty percent, only slightly less than at Beaumont-Hamel, although numbers fluctuate depending on the source. More than 150 prisoners of war were taken from the Newfoundland Regiment alone.

The Germans had recently introduced a new defensive strategy that saw the first lines of defence lightly manned, allowing the attackers to take the trenches with relative ease. It was designed to minimize casualties from concentrated British artillery and allow the German soldiers to engage in a fighting retreat, slowing down the attackers as reinforcements farther back prepared to launch a counterattack out of sight of artillery spotters. As the Newfoundlanders moved farther inward the distance between reinforcements and supplies grew. The Germans were waiting in the Bois du Sart and Bois

Stewart Hodder

Norman Way

William Harris

Clarence Wells

de Vert woods to outflank the attackers, forcing mass surrender (in the case of "D" Company) and carnage. The Germans had only partially introduced this elastic defence strategy along the Arras battle front at the time of the massive British offensive. According to some accounts, when Monchy was taken by the British on April 11, the elastic defence strategy was poorly implemented and aided in the fall of the village. As a result, the German commander was removed from the area and replaced by another who wholly supported the new system by the time the Newfoundlanders attacked on April 14.

Field Marshall Haig in his end of year dispatch referring to that day: "On other parts of our line heavy counter-attacks developed on the 14th April, the most violent of which were directed against Monchy-le-Preux."[25] However, the first sign of a counterattack did not occur until the men had already taken parts of Infantry Hill and were digging in on the downward slope a couple of hours after the attack was launched. At 7:30 a.m., two hours after zero hour, the Essex first reported the Germans massing on their left flank. By 9 a.m. what was left of Newfoundland's "D" Company was surrounded and captured. Ten brave souls attempted to flee; only one made it. Most of the men, if not all, who entered the two woods never returned. By 10 a.m., with both regiments annihilated, remnants of the Newfoundland Battalion Headquarters mustered men to fend off an initial German attack of some 200-300 soldiers.

Chesley Gladstone Arnold

If not for the fortitude and bravery of nine men from Newfoundland Battalion Headquarters and an Essex Regiment straggler, Monchy-le-Preux would have fallen back into German hands. Realizing that the Germans were forming a counterattack, twenty men of the Newfoundland Battalion Headquarters were gathered by their commanding officer, Lt. Col. Forbes-Robertson, within the ruined and heavily shelled village; they proceeded to the eastern edge of the town. Of those twenty, only nine managed to cover 100 yards of open ground to a raised hedge just behind the Assembly Trench, the attack's starting point in the morning; the others fell to machine gun, sniper and artillery fire. Initially these nine men, with bursts of rapid fire and later by carefully selecting their targets to conserve ammunition, forced the Germans to take cover. The German men targeted were mostly scouts and snipers. By killing the scouts, they kept the Germans guessing about the real numbers holding Monchy, as no reports could get back to the German command. A tenth man, temporarily knocked out, joined the others an hour and a half later. They managed to deceive the Germans into thinking they were a much larger force. Meanwhile the British held their ground much farther back behind Monchy, bracing for the inevitable German onslaught that never came. After four hours, a lull in the fighting allowed the commander to send a runner back to Brigade Headquarters

Monchy-le-Preux, Newfoundland Battlefield Memorial, c. 1925

Military Cross

to ask for reinforcements. They would come but not until after dark, although the British provided raking machine gun fire for their right flank and sporadic artillery support that "… must have killed a good many of our wounded lying out in the open & some collected in the Assembly trench."[26] A platoon of 2nd/Hampshires appeared in the village behind the ten men for support. It has been said that, if those ten men had failed, the British could have expected 40,000 more casualties to retake the village. To put that into perspective, the Canadians had suffered 10,000 casualties in taking Vimy Ridge only a few days earlier.

IT HAS BEEN SAID IF THOSE 10 MEN HAD FAILED, THE BRITISH COULD HAVE EXPECTED 40,000 MORE CASUALTIES TO RETAKE THE VILLAGE.

Heroes of Monchy: These nine Newfoundlanders saved Monchy-le-Preux from the counter-attacking Germans after the Newfoundland and Essex Regiments' advance failed. Three men later paid the supreme sacrifice and were added to the memorial to the missing at Beaumont-Hamel. All were decorated for this action.

Back Row: Albert.S.Rose D.C.M. M.M., *Walter Pitcher M.M. (Missing Masnieres), Lt. Col. James Forbes Robertson* V.C. M.C. *D.S.O., Kevin Keegan* M.C. & BAR, *Charles Parsons* M.M. & BAR, *Joseph Ross Waterfield* M.M. *(Missing Broembeek)*

Front Row: Frederick Curran M.M., *John H. Hillier* M.M., *Japheth Hounsell* M.M. *Missing Bailleul)*

CAPTAIN G. WHITTY, O.B.E., M.C. PHOTO ALBUM. COURTESY OF CAROLINE BALL

WINDMILL

Les Fosses Farm, April 23, 1917: The remnants of the Regiment were kept in the area and found themselves in support of another action led by the 4/Worcesters and 2nd/Hamshires of the 88th Brigade, just south of Monchy-le-Preux, an area that came to be known as Les Fosses Farm to the Newfoundlanders. The Regiment made up a composite battalion with the equally decimated Essex Regiment and were assigned to provide carrying parties and occupy the lines vacated by the two attacking battalions. They came under heavy artillery bombardment. Rupert Bartlett won his Military Cross during this action as he mustered troops from various units to defend the line from an ensuing German counterattack. The Regiment suffered more casualties, with 13 killed and 51 wounded. The names of the missing numbered 152 for both actions (11 from Les Fosses Farm), making Monchy-le-Preux the largest contributor to the memorial to the missing at the Newfoundland Memorial Park. Only approximately 11 men who died on the battlefield on April 14 have a known grave.

UNIDENTIFIED REGIMENT RETURNING FROM FRONT LINE

Waterfield's Military Medal (M.M.)

Death of Cyril Gardner

"Pte Squires Jumped in Shell hole [with] 2nd Lt when a shell exploded and killed or wounded seven men who were in it. He said 2 Lt killed by the same shell. Pte Squires is in Germany at present"

2nd Lt Clouston P.O.W[27]

Top: Arthur Penney (missing at Monchy) & Robin Stick

Harry Frampton

Sydney Smith

Alonzo Eddy (Adey)

3RD BATTLE OF YPRES (PASSCHENDAELE)

BATTLE OF LANGEMARCK (STEENBEEK)

The Royal Newfoundland Regiment spent many weeks on the Ypres/Flanders front line in 1916, 1917, and again in 1918. But it was in the 3rd Battle of Ypres, or Passchendaele, as it is more commonly known, that the unit squared off twice against the Germans in the infamous morass of mud. The first battle for the Regiment took place at Steenbeek and was known as the Battle of Langemarck. On the night of August 15, 1917, the Regiment took over the forward trenches near the Steenbeek River to the left of the Ypres-Staden Railway, southwest of the Belgian town of Langemarck. The Newfoundlanders, alongside the 2nd Battalion, Hampshire Regiment, were to lead the attack with the objective of taking the German line some 1000 yards ahead, which had been held by the enemy since the 1st Battle of Ypres in 1915. Several days leading up to the attack saw heavy rains, which thoroughly soaked the ground the men would have to drag themselves across. At 4:45 a.m. on August 16 the Newfoundland Regiment began the attack behind a creeping barrage, moving from muddy shell-hole to muddy shell-hole for cover. They faced little resistance except for periodic machine gun bursts coming from concrete pillboxes that slowed the advances but failed to halt them. From the *Newfoundland War Diary*: "A Large number of Germans were killed at the 1st objective. 2 Machine Guns were captured at the 1st objective, and 2 at the 2nd objective. Both objectives were immediately consolidated by digging trenches. The ground over which the Battle attacked was a mass of shell-holes and for the 2nd objective both Coys had to cross a swamp."[28] G.W.L. Nicholson described the swamp as a "quaking bog in which the men sank to their knees with every step."[29] Of the 508 men of all ranks who began the attack, 10 were killed or missing and 93 were wounded. Of the 93 wounded, 26 would succumb to wounds: 14 men killed at Steenbeek were denied a known burial and are now memorialized on the Beaumont-Hamel tablets. A few of them were killed by shell fire in the days leading up to the attack and one, 2nd Lieutenant Harold Barrett, M.M., for reasons lost to time, is also remembered on the Tyne Cot Memorial in Belgium, the only Newfoundlander, according to Sydney Frost, to have such an honour.[30] But even more curiously, Barrett's body was found, identified, and re-buried in Artillery Wood Cemetery in 1921, but according to official cemetery lists he is not there today.

Steenbeek, Belgium (Close to Ypres)

POELCAPELLE

Battle of Poelcapelle (Broembeek)

On October 9, 1917, the Regiment would be asked to attack again in the vicinity of Poelcapelle, starting near the secured 3rd objective from the Battle of Langemarck. Through heavy rain and fog and a dark night illuminated only by artillery bursts overhead, the "rain-sodden" Regiment made their way to the assembly point 300 yards short of the Broembeek River astride the Ypres-Staden Railway. The Newfoundlanders were assigned the 3rd objective some 2000 yards ahead and were supposed to advance on the third wave. Such were the conditions of the ground on which the attack was launched that the Newfoundland Regiment, who were only supposed to take the lead after the 2nd objective was reached and to push on to the 3rd objective, found themselves intermingled with the Worcester Regiment and leading the attack from the 1st objective on. The *War Diary*: "All objectives were gained without difficulty, except ... owing to machine-gun fire and sniping from pill-boxes ..."[31] Portions of the Regiment secured the 3rd objective but due to vicious German counterattacks and the withdrawal of

Martin Bertram Collins

ARTILLERY WOOD

a regiment on their left flank late in the day, the Newfoundlanders were forced to fall back 200 yards to consolidate their gains. Unlike the action at Steenbeek, the Regiment's losses were greater at Broembeek. The *War Diary* states 40 killed, 14 missing, 127 wounded; 6 died of wounds over the next few days, and 46 of those men are forever memorialized on the tablets. The most prominent loss, and one of the missing, was Captain James Allan Ledingham, commander of "A" Company, and one of the original commissioned officers of the Blue Puttees.

"We have found the body of Lieut. H.G. Barrett, M.M., and had it re-interred in Artillery Wood Cemetery, near Ypres."[32]

Horatius Seward (Horatio Seaward)

Leo Joseph Christopher

Fred Abbott

Stanley Goodyear

The Cloth Hall, Ypres, 1918

Dave Drake & George Emberley

Patrick O'Neill, Fermeuse
Regiment # 2263 K.I.A October 9, 1917
Broembeek.

Won Military Medal and the Battle of Langemarck (Steenbeek) August 16, 1917.

"In the attack on the enemy near Langemarck on the 16th August 1917, as company stretcher bearer during the advance showed great bravery and devotion to duty in bringing back wounded to the dressing station at Ruisseaux Farm. He personally took charge of the company stretcher bearers and had all cases cleared promptly."[33]

CAMBRAI: "THE GREAT EXPERIMENT"

After the Battle of Poelcapelle, the Regiment was on the move again. This time they were to take their place in another seminal battle that paved the way for future mechanized battles. The Germans learned from the British in this battle and developed Blitzkrieg strategies that were so effective at the outset of World War II. The aim: to launch a surprise attack on the German front and make an aggressive push deep into enemy lines with the hope of taking the strategic town of Cambrai away from the Germans. Two strategies new to the Germans were to be employed. First, the British wanted this to be a surprise attack; the artillery would not open up until the attack actually started. In the past they had bombarded the German lines with tons of artillery shells, hoping to waste the German trench system; in reality, all it did was let the Germans know they were coming. Besides, the Germans had built extensive concrete bunkers that the artillery shells could not break through. Second, it was the first time in battle that the tank would be used in a concerted effort. Before Cambrai, tanks were mostly used in individual or small groups, but never as the head of an attacking division with infantry following behind under cover. The tanks were to go ahead of the infantry and clear a way through the Hindenburg Line, a well-built defensive line

Fredrick White (left), Unknown (right)

Corbett Pitcher

Esau Baker

CAMBRAI, 1919

heavily fortified with concrete, by rolling over barbed wire and placing bails of lumber in trench openings so the tanks and infantry could cross over the top, as well as provide lateral machine gun fire from either side. Some tanks were also equipped with a single light artillery gun that could pack a wallop. It was the largest concentration of tanks brought together for one engagement and presented quite a sight bearing down on the Germans. From the German perspective, the end of the battle would involve a little ingenuity of their own in their use of shock troops or storm troopers. Military theorist and soldier Liddel Hart referred to Cambrai as "one of the landmarks in the history of warfare, the dawn of a new epoch."[34]

John Saunders

Hubert Oldford

Masnieres: November 20-22, 1917

Under cover of darkness and beneath huge camouflage nets, numerous divisions massed in preparation for this attack. The 29th Division's objective was to cross the St. Quentin Canal at Masnieres and Marcoing and secure both villages three and a half miles ahead of the starting point. The Newfoundland Regiment's objective was to take the bridge just left of Masnieres as well as the high ground just past the village. At 10:10 a.m. the bugle sounded for the Newfoundlanders to begin their assault. Initially it was "just a walk in the park," as one Newfoundlander described it.[35] It was not until the Battalion reached the outskirts of Les Rue Vertes that they experienced any real opposition from the Germans. "It was getting to the bridge that our real fighting commenced for we could see the Germans on the other side and they were firing on us for all they were worth with machine guns, and their snipers were as busy as could be."[36] The Newfoundlanders, with the aid of a lone tank, secured a footbridge that crossed the canal and led the 29th Division to the other side. They immediately came under heavy sniper and machine gun fire from nearby houses, suffering many casualties. "They had a machine gun up on the road and simply swept the one we were standing on with bullets and a lot of our men fell there killed and wounded. We fought on and drove them back and got up on part of the high ground before dark and then dug in for the night."[37] Having secured all that was asked of them, the Battalion spent a wet, cold, miserable night on the defensive flank of the 88th Brigade "as the village of Masnieres was not yet captured."[38]

The next day was spent in mopping up operations, clearing Masnieres of enemies, house by house, capturing 24 German prisoners while patrolling the canal bank. The Newfoundlanders were in defensive support when the Germans launched a beleaguered counterattack that was repulsed. While moving in columns through the village to shift positions, they were struck by an errant artillery shell that killed and wounded many,

MARCOING

including John Shiwak and Walter Pitcher, M.M., hero of Monchy-le-Preux. They spent the next day under cover in Masnieres before being relieved and marched to cellars in Marcoing west of the town. The next seven days were spent between the cellars of Marcoing, where the Germans relentlessly bombarded the town, and a stint in the front line between Marcoing and Masnieres on the German side of the canal.

"... FOR THE ENEMY WERE HID IN THE HOUSES AND BEGAN TO FIRE ON US FROM ALL DIRECTIONS AND IT WAS VERY DIFFICULT TO TELL WHERE ALL THE SHOTS WERE COMING FROM."[40]

Benjamin Benoit of Conne River was killed six days after joining the Battalion in the field November 20, 1917.

"Benoit – initial B – in B Company, was my pal. He came from Bay Despair in Placentia Bay –somewhere around there and was a furrier – trapping animals for their skins. He was killed in action on the Cambrai front on Nov. 20th. We were relieved on Nov 22nd. and I was out on a burying party and found Benoit and buried him just where he was lying. I took his paybook and gave it to our officer but cannot give the name of the place where Benoit was killed. He had a bullet right through his head. I recognize his number."

inf: Pte. H. Churchill 3682
No. Gen. Hosp. A.IV
Boulogne 13,4,18[39]

MASNIERES LOCK WHERE THE NEWFOUNDLANDERS CROSSED

CAPTAIN G. WHITTY, O.B.E., M.C. PHOTO ALBUM. COURTESY OF CAROLINE BALL

MARCOING: NOVEMBER 30 – DECEMBER 3, 1917

Rupert Bartlett

By November 29, the British Third Army had pushed as far as it would in this engagement. The tide was turning against them; not only were they unable to achieve their final objective, Cambrai, despite such a great opening day, but now the Germans were getting ready for a massive counterattack to regain ground lost in the previous week. The only ground held by the British on the north side of the canal was the narrow bridgehead around Masnieres established and held by the 29th Division, helped in no small part by the stalwart bravery of the Newfoundlanders, since the opening day of the battle.

On the morning of November 30, four British divisions lined the nine-mile front, while unbeknownst to the British, the Germans managed to amass nine. At 7 a.m. Marcoing was bombarded by high explosives and gas-filled artillery that only intensified as the morning wore on. The Newfoundland Regiment, along with the 88th Brigade, were preparing to re-enter the fray in Masnieres. Once they were ready to move, word came from command to the Brigade to find their own way to Masnieres to support the other two brigades of the 29th Division. Companies of the Newfoundland Battalion were ordered to rendezvous at the west end of Marcoing Copse, a small wood halfway between Marcoing and Les Rues Vertes. The heavy bombardment precluded any attempt by the 88th Brigade to gather en masse.

CAGNICOURT

RUINS OF THE MARCOING CHURCH, LOCATION OF NEWFOUNDLAND BATTALION HEADQUARTERS (CELLAR BENEATH)

The Newfoundland Regiment headed towards the Marcoing Copse, but instead of finding the 86th Brigade, the Newfoundlanders and other brigade battalions came across an advance party of German soldiers attempting to encircle the 29th Division in a bold, well-planned attack. The Newfoundland Regiment, resolute in their commitment to the task, lowered their bayonets and charged the advance party of German storm troopers in short quick bursts. Close hand-to-hand combat ensued and the Newfoundland Regiment, along with the regiments of Essex, Hampshire, Worcester, and 1st King's Own

Scottish Borderers, thwarted the German attempt to encircle the 29th Division. It was here that Captain Rupert Bartlett, brother to Arctic explorer Captain Bob Bartlett, fell leading his men in the charge.

As darkness fell, the 88th Brigade dug in along a stretch between the South Wales Borderers and Essex Regiment. The *War Diary* recorded: “Our strength in morning, 9 officers, 360 other ranks, at night, 8 officers, 230 other ranks.”[41] On that day alone the Regiment suffered one-third casualties.

Over the next 24 hours the Newfoundland Regiment came under heavy enemy sniper and machine gun fire. Other divisions were also coming under intense fire and in places the British defensive line was dangerously thin. The Newfoundlanders, along with the South Wales Borderers, were repositioned along a 2000-yard stretch between Marcoing and Les Rues Vertes that ran perpendicular to the canal just east of Marcoing Copse. Two battered Brigades that were holding a salient jutting out from Masnieres and Les Rue Vertes eastward were withdrawn and the salient abandoned. The British command, fearing complete annihilation of the 29th Division at Masnieres, ordered their retreat. The British Third Army could do little to protect them.

John Shiwak

The Newfoundlanders now occupied a position alongside the same lock that they had captured November 20 and were on the most advanced line of defence along this stretch. The Regiment would endure two more days of heavy bombardment, machine gun and sniper fire as the Germans fought hard to regain the initiative stymied by the tenacity of the sparse remnants of the Newfoundland Regiment.

Monday, December 3, 1917, turned out to be the fiercest day of fighting for the Regiment in the two-week battle. And its last. That morning the Germans made another massive push, with only the Newfoundland Regiment and the South Wales Borderers standing between a German rout of the British at Marcoing.

Eyewitness Report:

“… Nov. 30th he commenced to bombard us and attack and I can tell you we lived in perfect hell for that day. About 7 in the morning he commenced his attack and began to shell the village frightfully. I shall never forget it. About 10 am it reached the height of its intensity and it was something awful. Nothing but houses falling all around us bang, crash, bang powder and smoke all around us. In the midst of it all we were suddenly ordered out as the Boches [Germans] were attacking over our right and we had to meet them … we met the Germans just outside [Les Rues Vertes] and on our side of the canal and then we had to fight.”[42]

British Soldiers in shallow cover during the Battle of Cambrai

At 7 a.m. a great barrage of artillery shells and trench mortars came raining down on the bunkered Newfoundlanders. As the morning wore on, the German artillery landed with deadly accuracy. The dead began to pile up in the trenches and outposts as waves of German infantry came along the valley of the canal. Sometime during the morning the Newfoundland Regiment were forced to relinquish portions of the trench to the advancing German infantry. By noon, Brigadier Nelson reported the "South Wales Borderers and the Newfoundland Regiment almost wiped out by shellfire."[43] Despite the heavy losses, another 71 men were killed, wounded, or taken prisoner; the depleted ranks of the Newfoundland Regiment continued to hold back the Germans. Though they were finally relieved at nine that night, the Regiment had foiled the German attempt to take Marcoing. Joseph Babstock recorded in his diary: "Captured Dec 3rd, at noon after a terrific bombardment by the germans many dead in the trench …"[44]

DIVISONAL COL

December 4, 1917, General Byng ordered the withdrawal of British forces back to the Hindenburg Support Line to settle down for the winter, thus relinquishing Marcoing and Bourlon Wood, which had been won and held at a great human cost. The end result of such a promising offensive on November 20 turned into a debacle by December 4. The British suffered over 40,000 casualties and the Germans 45,000. The Newfoundland Regiment would take months to recover. They lost two-thirds of their number to casualties.

Fifty soldiers from this engagement have no known graves. Seventeen of the missing men were a result of the initial two days of attacks launched on November 20; at least two, John Shiwak and Walter Pitcher, were killed and buried on the 21st, and there were perhaps eight more buried at the same time whose graves were lost in the subsequent horror of war. Very few of the men who died during the attack on November 20 were listed as missing. Ten actually died in the artillery shell burst on November 21. The majority of men who died on November 20 are buried in the Marcoing Cemetery, perhaps a testament to Padre Thomas Nangle, who came up from reserves to bury Newfoundland's dead who were scattered around the lock and the road on the German side of the canal. Thirty-three of the men went missing in the defensive action that took place from November 30 through December 3. Rupert Bartlett disappeared on the November 30 charge from Marcoing. Most men, however, were killed in the massive German counterattack on the morning of December 3, including George Ricketts, Tommy Ricketts' brother. Very few of the men who died on December 3 have a known grave. Only two may have died during the battle and have a headstone; a handful of others died of wounds, and twenty-three were captured. Many were simply buried by German trench mortars and artillery. At least one, George Kane, was captured wounded, died in captivity, and was buried in the nearby Seranvilles Cemetery in an unmarked grave.

Dorman Butt

Neville Samson

LECTING POST

EYEWITNESS ACCOUNTS:

"We stayed in our positions being shelled heavenly every day until they made another big counter attack on Dec 3rd and by sheer weight of numbers and shells fire drove some of our troops on our left and right back. However we hung on we could see the enemy coming on towards us in masses. We managed to hold them, however but for a while during that awful afternoon thought that my last hour had come."[45]

Joseph Babstock: "On the morning of the German counter attack they bombarded us with Trench mortars and Field Guns and levelled our trenches and killed or wounded nearly all the men in our sector of the trench."[46]

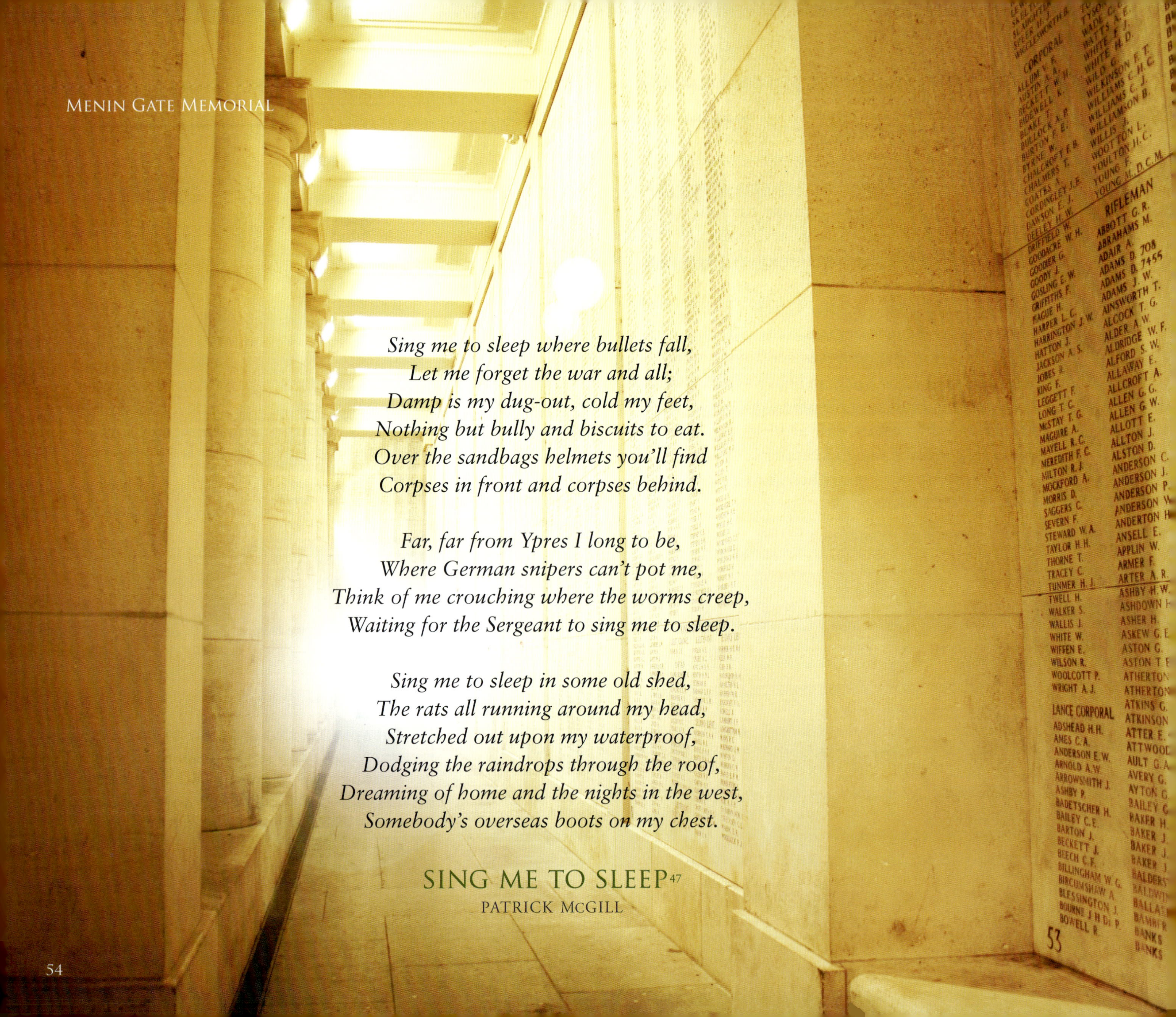

Sing me to sleep where bullets fall,
Let me forget the war and all;
Damp is my dug-out, cold my feet,
Nothing but bully and biscuits to eat.
Over the sandbags helmets you'll find
Corpses in front and corpses behind.

Far, far from Ypres I long to be,
Where German snipers can't pot me,
Think of me crouching where the worms creep,
Waiting for the Sergeant to sing me to sleep.

Sing me to sleep in some old shed,
The rats all running around my head,
Stretched out upon my waterproof,
Dodging the raindrops through the roof,
Dreaming of home and the nights in the west,
Somebody's overseas boots on my chest.

SING ME TO SLEEP[47]

PATRICK McGILL

1918: The Final Year

Ypres – Passchendaele 1918

The Battalion ranks were so depleted after the long engagement at Cambrai in late 1917 that the remnants of the unit were reorganized into two companies. Number 1 Company comprised the men of the former "A" and "B" Companies, and the Number 2 Company included the old "C" and "D" Companies. From January until March 1918, the Regiment found itself moving around the Passchendaele sector, performing work details, digging trenches, laying wire, building tramways, and occasionally taking over firing lines a week at a time. Not much had changed in the three months they were away from this sector, as the mud, water-filled shell-holes, and shallow trenches dominated the landscape. In no man's land the dead of "friend and foe" from the Battle of Passchendaele lay unburied, months after the engagement officially ended. The Newfoundlanders suffered some casualties during this time, including 17 killed, 3 missing in action, and 66 wounded; 14 names of those men who died before March 30, 1918, eventually found their way on the memorial tablets.

In January 1918, King George V bestowed the title Royal to the Newfoundland Regiment, marking only the third time in the history of Great Britain that such an honour was bestowed on an active regiment in the field. It was the only such occurrence in World War I.

Letter from Field Marshall Douglas Haig to 1st Battalion Royal Newfoundland Regiment Commander Colonel Woodruffe:[48]

> Feby 4th 1918
>
> Dear Colonel Woodruffe.
>
> I have much pleasure in informing you that his Majesty the King, in view of the magnificent bravery and resolute determination shown by all ranks, has been graciously pleased to approve of the grant of the title 'Royal' to the Newfoundland Regt. Please accept and convey to all ranks my warmest Congratulations that your achievements have met with such well-earned recognition. Official intimation will be sent you, and this is merely a personal message from myself to your gallant Regiment.
>
> Yours very truly
> (sgd) D. Haig

YPRES RESEVOIR

Bailleul

Bailleul 1918

The Germans prepared a massive spring offensive along great swaths of the Western Front in an effort to break the back of the Allied resistance before the Americans could mobilize in force. The Germans began the offensive on the Somme March 21, 1918, and carried through until April 4, penetrating farther into the French countryside, deeper than at any other time during the war. On April 9 the Germans launched their second offensive, known as the Lys Offensive, along the Belgium-France border. The Newfoundlanders were on their way with the 88th Brigade, as the 29th Division had been ordered back to the Somme front when the Germans launched the offensive in Flanders. The Brigade disembarked and was immediately thrown into defensive positions near Bailleul in northern France. From April 10-14, the Battalion fought a series of battles, trying to slow down the German onslaught as the British retreated to higher ground north of Bailleul.

NEW IRISH FARM

Ephraim King

MEN OF THE ROYAL NEWFOUNDLAND REGIMENT RESTING IN THE SNOW BETWEEN HESDIN AND FRESSIN, DECEMBER 20, 1917

On April 10, the diverted Battalion found itself in the midst of chaos at Les Creche east of Bailleul as refugees pushing wheelbarrows stuffed with belongings, "war wagons," guns, and wounded competed for space in retreat of the advancing Germans. The first casualties were suffered by the Battalion as they approached machine gun posts at the Steenwerck Railway Station. Field Marshall Haig on April 11 ordered, "Every position must be held to the last man: there must be no retirement. With our backs to the wall and believing in the justice of our cause, each one of us must fight on to the end."[49] On April 12, a day of crisis, the Battalion fought along a number of fronts, suffering heavy casualties. By evening, the unit, under protection of a low railway embankment "and prepared to fight to a finish,"[50] picked off German soldiers advancing in what would later be called "a brilliant counterattack."[51] On April 13, the Battalion offered "stubborn resistance put up during the retirement to the Bailleul-Crucifix Line ... saved a serious situation"[52] that allowed the 34th Division (88th Brigade temporarily under their command) to retreat to Ravelsburg Heights. The Newfoundlanders held the line until the way was clear and were the last to reach the Heights.

A total of 45 names on the tablets can be attributed to the Battle of Bailleul, missing from April 10-14. They included Gordon Tizzard, missing on the 10th, Hubert Webber, missing on the 14th, and Japhett Hounsell, M.M., hero of Monchy-le-Preux, who was lost on April 12.

After Bailleul the Regiment was removed from the 29th Division and attached to General Headquarters for a period of rebuilding.

BUCKINGHAM PALACE.

I join with my grateful people in sending you this memorial of a brave life given for others in the Great War. [54]

George R.I.

DEATH OF MAURICE GREGORY CONNORS, APRIL 12, 1918:

"I think he was in 'A' Coy. at the time of his casualty he was clean shaven; he had a gold tooth in his upper jaw which could be plainly seen when his mouth was open; he was about 5'6" or 7", slightly made; he joined with me about a month before. I did not know him very well.

"We were on the Armentieres front and retiring from Bailleul about 4.0.p.m. I passed his body before we had entirely got out of the village as there were houses on both sides. He was quite dead but did not look knocked about at all. We passed on."

Pte. Wm. Tremblett, 3575[53]

"... I WISH TO PLACE ON RECORD MY VERY GREAT REGRET AT THEIR WITHDRAWAL FROM A DIVISION IN WHICH THEY HAVE SERVED SO LONG AND BRILLIANTLY ... THE BATTALION HAS SHOWN ITSELF TO BE, UNDER ALL CIRCUMSTANCES OF GOOD AND BAD FORTUNE, A SPLENDID FIGHTING UNIT ... THEY CAN LOOK BACK ON A RECORD OF WHICH THEY AND THEIR FELLOW COUNTRYMEN HAVE EVERY RIGHT TO BE PROUD."[55]

The Final Push: 1918

Clarence Harris

After spending the summer in Ecuries providing guard duty to General Headquarters and rebuilding their ranks from new recruits, the Battalion was ordered to join the 9th Scottish Division on September 13. The men were disappointed to discover they would not be rejoining the 29th Division. On September 12 they entrained for Esquelbecq, Belgium, and the next day, Friday the 13th, joined the 28th Brigade of the 9th Division. They entered the front line for the first time in months on September 20, 2000 yards behind a trench they had occupied back in 1916. Despite returning to the madness of the Ypres battlefield, grounds familiar to many in the Regiment (half had never seen action), there was a sense of optimism building among the ranks that the upcoming "Push" would finally put an end to this brutal war. What began as a series of attacks and battles, which consumed men and equipment at an alarming rate, ended in Armistice six weeks later.

DRURY CRUCIFIX

Charles Hobbs

Keiberg Ridge: Sept 28-29, 1918

The first attack came on the morning of September 28; 9th Division Brigadier-General J.L. "Mad" Jack addressed the 28th Brigade: "... has heard of your gallantry, has seen your smartness, and prays you use your wits ..."[56] The Newfoundlanders played a support role but the next day led an attack on Keiberg Ridge. With no objectives given, the Battalion moved forward in rushes against heavy artillery and machine guns amidst "considerable resistance" from the Germans. By that evening the advance came to a halt and the British were in command of the Ridge. The Battalion advanced over nine miles, leaving the treacherous Flanders mud for the green rolling hills of Belgian farmland. They suffered a total of 144 casualties, 38 due to sickness brought on by the heavy rains and cold; 92 were wounded, 14 killed or missing, and of those, 5 men are today commemorated on the Beaumont-Hamel memorial to the missing.

Within days the Regiment was advancing again. October became a series of forward movements with two larger battles within. The Germans were retreating, but put up dogged resistance to the end. Casualties happened on a daily basis and some of those who died were lost in the tumult. On October 2, the Newfoundlanders were in the vicinity of Ledeghem when they were involved in stopping a half-hearted German counterattack.

Richard Joseph Hamen

Battle of Courtrai (Ledeghem): October 14-20, 1918

On October 14, the Battalion was in the midst of another advance. Under heavy smoke and fog, with visibility on the ground reduced to two yards, the unit advanced, taking about 500 prisoners, 8 guns, and more than 100 machine guns from the enemy. "The advance was done entirely by compass bearings and a large number of prisoners were captured in cellars and pill boxes without showing any fight. One platoon alone captured 34 machine guns and in one case a Coy. Commander walked right on to and fell over an enemy machine gun and gunners."[57] "D" Company suffered heavy casualties when they stumbled upon an enemy battery of field guns that promptly opened up on them at point-blank range. More casualties were suffered when the men had to cross the Wulfdambeek stream; some of the men were picked off while in the water. On October 15, the Regiment continued their advance under little opposition until they reached the River Lys. After a few days rest, the 28th Brigade crossed the River Lys on October 20, and by the afternoon had encountered stiff opposition at the railway at Vichte, suffering many casualties. The Battalion was given a few days rest.

Ingoyghem: October 25-26, 1918

In the early morning on October 25, "D" Company was struck by an artillery shell in their billets that caused a fire and seven casualties. The Regiment, who had gone back in the field in September with a full battalion complement, were, in five weeks, reduced to less than half that number. Until they formed up to advance on Ingoyghem, the Regiment had been shelled heavily by the Germans. They advanced to Ingoyghem and pushed on through until they came across heavy machine gun fire. At this point the Regiment dug in, as an advance from here would be murderous. The Regiment undertook patrol duties the next day only to find out that the Germans had not retreated in this sector. They spent the day under heavy artillery and machine gun fire until they were relieved in the line that evening.

For the Regiment the hard fighting was over. Through the month of October the official *War Diary* recorded 334 casualties of all ranks, including 41 killed, 171 wounded, 15 missing, and another 102 reported sick. Many gallantry awards were issued, including 2 Military Crosses, 1 Bar to the Military Cross, 7 Distinguished Conduct Medals, 16 Military Medals, 2 Bars to Military Medals, and the Newfoundland Regiment's first and only Victoria Cross, awarded to Tommy Ricketts. Twenty-one men who lost their lives during the month of October are commemorated on the Beaumont-Hamel Memorial Tablets.

Presentation of medals by Newfoundland's Minister of Militia, J.R. Bennett, won at the Battle of Bailleul, Ecuries, June 1918

On November 11, 1918, the official *War Diary* simply stated "No Parade owing Germans signing Armistice." The war was over.

The Newfoundland Royal Naval Reserve

Sampson Brown, a Reservist who survived the war

The Newfoundland Royal Naval Reserve Tablet sits on the left of the Regiment's. Continuing the proud seafaring tradition, many Newfoundlanders signed up for the Newfoundland Royal Naval Reserve. Some men were trained and in reserve long before the outbreak of hostilities, having been reservists on the HMS *Calypso* stationed in St. John's. The term of enlistment was for five years and recruits had to do 28 days of training each year. The *Calypso*, built in 1883 and renamed the HMS *Briton* in 1916, had been commissioned as a naval reserve vessel in 1902 specifically to train and retain young men for the Newfoundland Royal Naval Reserve and was one of the last steel-hulled, steam and sail, three-masted barques built for the Royal Navy. These men served on many types of vessels, from converted fishing trawlers and minesweepers, commandeered ocean liners and true battleships. The first Newfoundlanders to set foot in Gallipoli were from the Newfoundland Royal Naval Reserve, who witnessed and partook in the landings in early 1915 and were there to ferry the last evacuees from Cape Helles in January 1916. They served alongside the Royal Navy and were known as the world's best small-boat men. The Royal Navy recognized the value that small-boat fishermen of Newfoundland could offer to the Navy in the late 1800s. Small-boat boarding parties were needed to traverse the sometimes rough seas of the open ocean to inspect potential enemy ships, and no better seafaring race for the job could be found than the hardy Newfoundland fisherman or sailor.

When war ensued, the trained reservists were ready for action. A total of 1964 men served with the Newfoundland Royal Naval Reserve; 180 paid the supreme sacrifice. They were dispersed

"... the Newfoundland Royal Naval Reserve, which was composed of fishermen who spend their lives in the cod schooners and sealing in the Arctic. They are splendid, hearty people, the finest small-ship seamen in the world ... Many will remember the armed merchantmen of the Tenth Squadron which were engaged in the German Blockade ... Their duties necessitated boarding suspicious vessels in all sorts of weather. These Newfoundland fishermen to a great extent formed the boats' crews who carried out this arduous and dangerous work."[58]

Bowring Park Replica Tablet, Unveiling Day, July 1, 2009

Newfoundland Royal Navy Reservists in front of the HMS Calypso

George Stringer

throughout the Royal Navy and the 114 men listed on the Newfoundland Royal Naval Reserve Tablet served on more than 30 vessels. Major losses happened on the HMS *Viknor*, *Laurentic*, *Alcantara*, *Bayano*, and *Clan McNaughton*.

The HMS *Viknor* went down January 13, 1915, with all hands. This vessel was in heavy seas not far from where the *Laurentic* would end her days, and it is believed that she struck a newly laid German mine, taking almost 300 lives; 24 Newfoundlanders are commemorated on the tablets at Beaumont-Hamel. The sinking of the *Viknor* represents the largest loss to Newfoundland families up to that point in the war.

HMS *Clan McNaughton* was another vessel that sank with all hands, within a month of the *Viknor*, taking 281 men with her, including 22 Newfoundland Royal Naval Reservists who are all remembered on the tablet. One British seaman lost on the *McNaughton* wrote a letter home before she set sail for the last time, fearing that it would be his last voyage, as the extra guns and armour recently added made her top-heavy. The day she sank the *McNaughton* was in heavy seas.

Walter Spurrell of Trouty was a victim of a German war crime when he was lost on the SS *Torrington* in the Mediterranean. Sunk by German U-boat U55, the captain and the crew were picked up by the U-boat. The captain was taken prisoner and brought below, the hatches sealed, and the U-boat submerged, murdering the entire crew, save for the captain. After the war, the U-boat commander, Wilhelm Werner, fled Germany, avoiding war crimes trials that were taking place at Leipzig, as he was one of three U-boat commanders sought by the British.

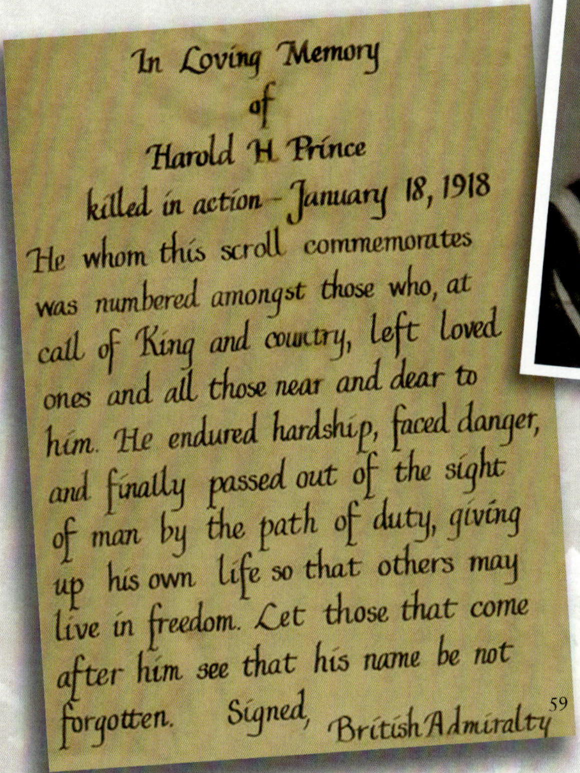

In Loving Memory
of
Harold H. Prince
killed in action - January 18, 1918
He whom this scroll commemorates was numbered amongst those who, at call of King and country, left loved ones and all those near and dear to him. He endured hardship, faced danger, and finally passed out of the sight of man by the path of duty, giving up his own life so that others may live in freedom. Let those that come after him see that his name be not forgotten. Signed, British Admiralty[59]

Harold Prince

Edward Smart

John Walter Dyke

Simeon Whalen

HMS Viknor

The Alcantara *in battle with the* Grief

Seventy-two men of Port de Grave electoral district volunteered for the Newfoundland Royal Naval Reserve. On February 29, 1916, the H.M.S. *Alcantara*, an armed merchant cruiser, sank after an old-fashioned broadside slugfest with the German armed merchantman, the *Grief*. At 8:45 on that fateful morning, lookouts on the *Alcantara* reported smoke in the distance. On investigation, the *Alcantara* came across the *Grief*, which was disguised as a Norwegian merchant ship en route from Trondheim, Norway, for Rio de Janeiro. After closing in, the captain ordered a boarding party over the sides; at that moment the *Grief* dropped its bulwark, unveiled its guns, and fired, hitting the bridge and drawing first casualties. Nathan Mugford, while launching a boat over the sides, was mortally wounded and fell into the sea. Nathan's wounds were horrific; with no hope of his survival, an officer ordered him euthanized. Both vessels managed to maul each other below the waterline with numerous hits, until they had to be abandoned. Nathan's girlfriend, Maude Beecham, always claimed that one night while lying in bed with her mother, she opened her eyes and Nathan was in the room. When she woke her mother, Nathan was gone, and her mother said she would "… see Nathan no more."[60]

Nathan Mugford

THE STORY WAS BROUGHT HOME THAT NATHAN WAS EUTHANIZED BY AN OFFICER, AS HIS WOUNDS WERE HORRIFIC AND THERE WAS NO HOPE OF SURVIVAL.

There were twelve Newfoundlanders on the *Alcantara*, and four came from Port de Grave. Two survived, two died in this engagement, and only one would survive the war. Nathan Mugford and William Henry Dawe were killed; Alfred A. Andrews and John Charles Tucker survived. Tucker would lose his life on the HMS *Laurentic* in 1917 on his way home on furlough.

The *Laurentic* struck a mine off Malin Head, Ireland, January 25, 1917, while en route from Liverpool to Halifax with many passengers from the Newfoundland Royal Naval Reserve returning home for a period of rest. Of the fifteen lifeboats that were launched, only the men in seven survived the frigid North Atlantic. Many were found frozen at the oars; Tucker is said to have been on a lifeboat that got caught up in the screw as the *Laurentic* was slipping beneath the waves. Of the twenty-two Newfoundlanders on the *Laurentic*, seventeen have been memorialized on the Beaumont-Hamel tablets, two are buried in Ireland, and one serving with the Royal Naval Reserve is commemorated elsewhere. There were two known survivors from Newfoundland. The *Laurentic* was also carrying a hefty payload of gold bullion, sparking a salvage operation immediately after the war that has continued to this day as treasure hunters attempt to find the last few unaccounted gold bars.

The Calypso *in full sail*

John Tucker

HMS Laurentic

Recruits on St. John's dock in front of H.M.S Calypso/Briton

William Henry Dawe

Presented to Josiah Porter
by his mother with sincere
love & earnest Prayer
for his eternal & everlasting
welfare
through waves & clouds & Storm
Gods power will Clear thy way
wait his time the darkest night
will end in brightest day

The Corsican

ARMISTICE

November 11, 1918, at 11 a.m. the First World War officially came to an end. More than four years had passed since it began. The war involved 23 countries around the globe, led to millions of young men being slaughtered, as well as countless amputees and scarred lives.

The first Newfoundlanders to return home from the Regiment were the recently released POWs, wounded, and a few select others, including the Royal Newfoundland Regiment's only Victoria Cross winner, Tommy Ricketts. They arrived in St. John's to much fanfare on February 7, 1919, on the "good ship" *Corsican*. The return to civilian life for the first returning draft had now commenced. The ever-present carnage, noise, brutality, mud, dread, sleepless nights, cold, wet, cruelty, fear, terror, horror, rats, decomposing flesh, stench, lice, and death were now behind them and existed only in their dreams.

There were more than 16 million dead: nearly 10 million were military; another 6.5 million were civilians who died of war-related famine and disease. In many countries around the world November 11 is revered and honoured every year, and those lost in all wars are remembered on this date. The symbol most often used is the poppy immortalized in the poem by John McCrae, "In Flanders Fields." Newfoundland chose the forget-me-not, a small blue flower, but over the years the poppy has superseded it.

The effects of millions of demobilized military volunteers, many of them so badly injured they were unable to work, were devastating to many of the countries they were returning to. Empires fell as the war ended, civil war ensued in Russia and Turkey, and Germany saw record inflation. Newfoundland was unable to support her returning

MARBLE MONUMENT TO REGIMENT SOLDIERS, BAY ROBERTS, NL

soldiers and many of the healthy ones left for the United States. All around the world the effects of the war were far-reaching: the old Empires crumbled, and socialism, communism, and fascism began to take root. Empire building took on new ugly tones and reared its head as ultra-nationalism or despotism. The closing of the war opened the door for the Second World War twenty-one years later. To this day the effects of the first terrible war still resonate throughout the globe. The conflicts in the former Yugoslavia, the breakup of Czechoslovakia, the war in Iraq, and the underlying seething hatred that still permeates the dismantled Austro-Hungarian, Russian, and Turkish Empires all have their start in the aftermath of the First World War or are continuations of the hatred that spurred the war in the first place.

Demobilization Card

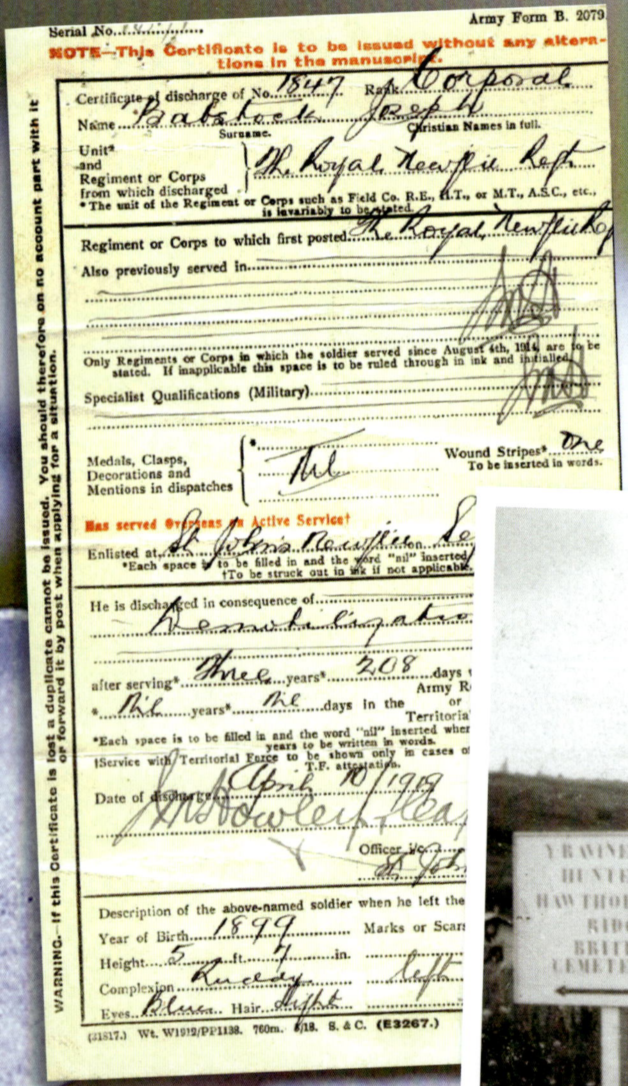

Serial No. .... Army Form B. 2079.

NOTE—This Certificate is to be issued without any alterations in the manuscript.

Certificate of discharge of No. 1847 Rank Corporal

Name Babstock Joseph — Surname. Christian Names in full.

Unit* and Regiment or Corps from which discharged: The Royal Newfld Regt

*The unit of the Regiment or Corps such as Field Co. R.E., H.T., or M.T., A.S.C., etc., is invariably to be stated.

Regiment or Corps to which first posted: The Royal Newfld

Also previously served in ....

Only Regiments or Corps in which the soldier served since August 4th, 1914 are to be stated. If inapplicable this space is to be ruled through in ink and initialled.

Specialist Qualifications (Military) ....

Medals, Clasps, Decorations and Mentions in dispatches: Nil

Wound Stripes*: One — To be inserted in words.

Has served Overseas on Active Service†

Enlisted at St. John's Newfoundland

*Each space is to be filled in and the word "nil" inserted. †To be struck out in ink if not applicable.

He is discharged in consequence of Demobilization

after serving* three years* 208 days with the Colours, and* nil years* nil days in the Army Reserve or Territorial Force

*Each space is to be filled in and the word "nil" inserted where necessary; number of years to be written in words.

†Service with Territorial Force to be shown only in cases of T.F. attestation.

Date of discharge April 10/1919

Officer i/c .... St. John's

Description of the above-named soldier when he left the Colours.

Year of Birth 1899 — Marks or Scars: left ...

Height 5 ft. 7 in.

Complexion Ruddy

Eyes Blue Hair light

WARNING.—If this Certificate is lost a duplicate cannot be issued. You should therefore on no account part with it or forward it by post when applying for a situation.

(31817.) Wt. W1919/PP1138. 750m. 8/18. S. & C. (E3267.)

Near the entrance to Newfoundland Memorial Park, Beaumont-Hamel, France, 1920s

Burying the Dead

There are various reasons why these men are on Newfoundland's memorial to the missing. For the Newfoundland Royal Naval Reserve and the Newfoundland Mercantile Marine, it is not often the ocean gives up her dead. But for the men of the Royal Newfoundland Regiment the reasons they remain missing vary. Some may have been blown to pieces by direct artillery or trench mortar blasts. Others went over the top and were cut down in no man's land or lay there wounded for days until they succumbed to their injuries. The Newfoundland War Memorial Park at Beaumont-Hamel is one big graveyard where many soldiers lie just beneath the surface. In Flanders Fields, which, ironically, only briefly resembled a field during the war, many men were swallowed up in the quagmire of mud and water-filled shell-holes, sometimes simply by a misstep while coming to or from the front in the darkness. And yet others were literally buried alive in the tumult of cascading turf from high explosive shells that could send debris 100 feet into the air.

SERRE ROAD NO.1

During the war, burial units would move into captured territory and begin the process of burying the bodies in concentrated cemeteries like Hawthorn Ridge Cemetery No. 2 inside the Newfoundland Memorial Park. When Beaumont-Hamel finally fell in November 1916, the soldiers set about burying their dead, and amongst them were soldiers who had lain out in the field since July 1. The task undertaken was gruesome, one that traumatized the already shaken British soldiers. After the war, Padre Thomas Nangle, Newfoundland's representative on the Imperial War Graves Commission, while spear-heading the purchase, design, and construction of memorials for Newfoundland, also led reburial parties to search for Newfoundland's fallen, to identify and place them in concentrated cemeteries. Nangle asked the prime minister,

Exhuming graves of Newfoundlanders near the Masnieres lock captured by Regiment on November 20, 1917

CAPTAIN G. WHITTY, O.B.E., M.C. PHOTO ALBUM.
COURTESY OF CAROLINE BALL

Sir Richard Squires, to recommend three of his party for the Order of the British Empire (OBE), a newly formed award to recognize those who performed exceptionally in a military or civilian role. James Lambert, John Lawrence Murphy, and William Brown were never given that recognition.

Not all the men who were missing resulted from being left on the battlefield or blown to pieces by artillery or trench mortar; some were buried. We know the exact burial location of a few of these men. There are specific references in trench maps used at the time of their deaths. Some others were buried by the Germans, their identity tags removed and sent via the Red Cross so British authorities could record their deaths. Others were buried by their comrades, burial location noted and marked. Later, when Padre Nangle and his crew came to exhume the body, their identity disks would have rotted away or been returned by British or German burial parties at the time of death, and thus they joined the ranks of the missing. Sometimes war would return, time and time again, among the fields of Flanders and the Somme, obliterating burial sites and hastily dug graves. As many as 128 headstones peppered throughout Commonwealth War Grave cemeteries in France and Belgium have the Caribou crest, and the inscription reads "Known unto God." The names of those cemeteries and identified burial locations are scattered throughout the pages of this book.

The largest number of unidentified Newfoundland Regiment soldiers lie in the large Serre Road No. 2 Cemetery near Beaumont-Hamel. Cemeteries were built, like Hawthorne Ridge No. 2, within the Newfoundland Memorial Park, where men identified only by their brass buttons, collar dogs, or brass regiment insignia attached to epaulets, and those known to be buried have headstones laid down shoulder to shoulder with no space in between. Except for a few headstones in the front that were added later, the two long rows indicate that the men were buried in two purposely built trenches.

There are a few instances where the cemetery is known, but for reasons unknown, the men were not found after the war. Horatius (Horatio) Seward (Seaward) had exact burial co-ordinates at Broembeek; "Blue Puttee" George Kane, amongst others, was captured at Marcoing on December 3, 1917, and later died of wounds in German hands. The Germans reported he was buried at Seranvilles Cemetery near Cambrai and the tags returned to the Red Cross. Maurice Gregory Connors was also buried by the Germans, but the location was not recorded. The Germans often gave proper burials to the dead from both sides; however, many of those buried by the Germans still ended up on the memorial to the missing as their burial locations were lost in the confusion of war.

Of the 592 missing men of the Royal Newfoundland Regiment only 128 have been buried as unidentified Newfoundland soldiers of the Great War. There are still 464 who are lying out in farmers' fields or underneath roadways or beneath a headstone simply marked "A British soldier of the Great War known unto God," identified only by the tattered remnants of a khaki uniform or completely obliterated by the modernization and efficiency of the Great War. For a grieving mother it is a difficult cross to bear, knowing that your beloved son has died with no known grave, and that closure does not come for the broken-hearted. Even though Newfoundland, by its relationship with the sea, was no stranger to her sons dying with no known grave, the impact on families was greatly felt even to this day.

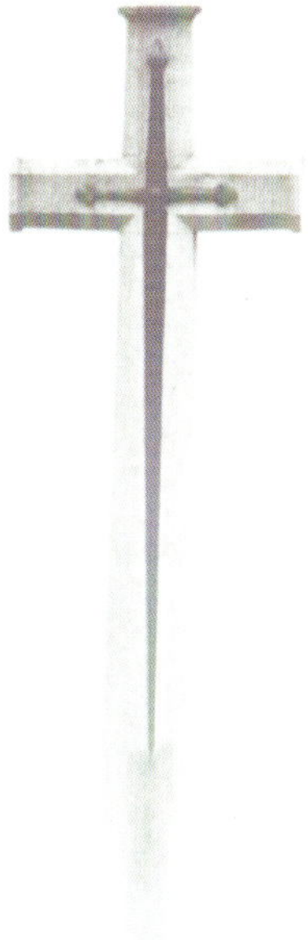

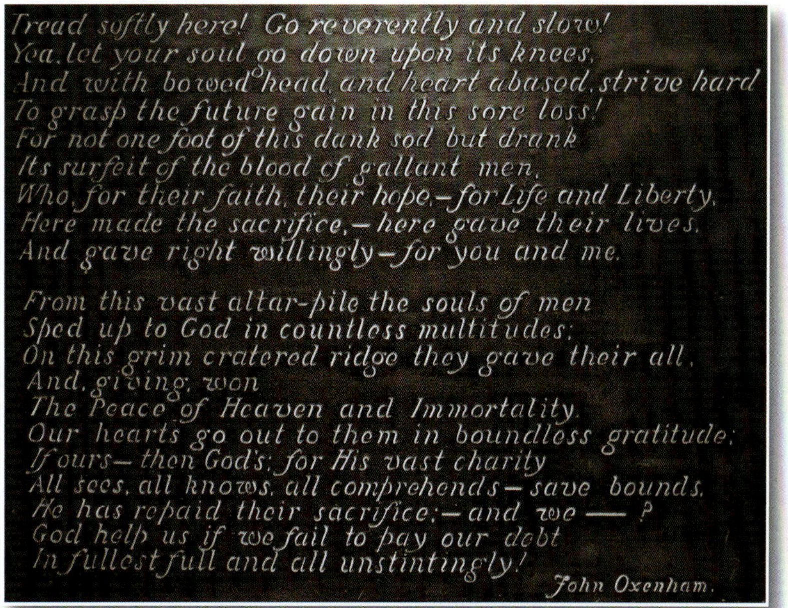

Tread softly here! Go reverently and slow!
Yea, let your soul go down upon its knees,
And with bowed head, and heart abased, strive hard
To grasp the future gain in this sore loss!
For not one foot of this dank sod but drank
Its surfeit of the blood of gallant men,
Who for their faith, their hope,—for Life and Liberty,
Here made the sacrifice,—here gave their lives,
And gave right willingly—for you and me.

From this vast altar-pile the souls of men
Sped up to God in countless multitudes;
On this grim cratered ridge they gave their all,
And, giving, won
The Peace of Heaven and Immortality.
Our hearts go out to them in boundless gratitude;
If ours—then God's; for His vast charity
All sees, all knows, all comprehends—save bounds.
He has repaid their sacrifice;—and we—?
God help us if we fail to pay our debt
In fullest full and all unstintingly!

John Oxenham.

"... ABOUT THE FIRST DEAD MAN I CAME TO WAS ONE OF THE BOYS. I COULD NOT RECOGNIZE HIM BECAUSE HE HAD BEEN HIT IN THE HEAD ... WE ALSO BURIED HIM AND PUT A CROSS TO MARK HIS GRAVE ... HE WAS A SENIOR GUNNER AND HE DIED WITH HIS [LEWIS - MACHINE] GUN ON HIS SHOULDER, LIKE A SOLDIER AND A BRAVE MAN ... HE HAD A PHOTO OF HIS SISTER IN HIS HAND, AND WE REVERENTLY LAID HIM TO REST WITH IT ..." [61]

SERRE ROAD NO. 2

Charles McCarthy

BURIED AT SEA

There are eleven members listed on the Royal Newfoundland Regiment Tablet who were buried at sea. Some were on hospital ships off the Gallipoli Peninsula when they died and were handed over to the briny ocean. They are John Hardy, Joachim Murphy, who was wounded at Caribou Hill, Frederick Charles Somerton, Morley Soper, Walter Tucker, John Francis Viscount, and William Patrick Miller, whose father was killed with the 24th Regiment in the Zulu Wars of 1879. Four members of the Regiment were buried at sea while crossing the Atlantic. One man, Jabez William King of Lewisporte, died before joining the 2nd Battalion in Ayr, Scotland. He left

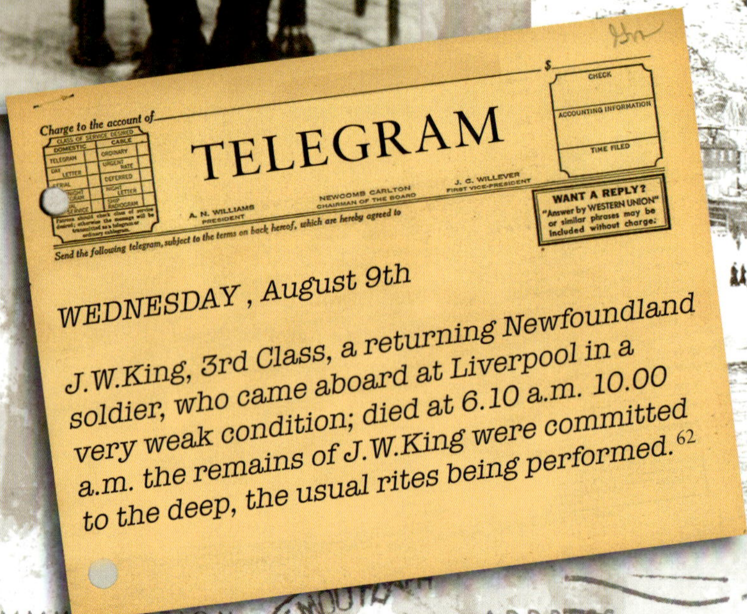

Charge to the account of

TELEGRAM

A. N. WILLIAMS, PRESIDENT — NEWCOMB CARLTON, CHAIRMAN OF THE BOARD — J. C. WILLEVER, FIRST VICE-PRESIDENT

WANT A REPLY? "Answer by WESTERN UNION" or similar phrases may be included without charge.

Send the following telegram, subject to the terms on back hereof, which are hereby agreed to

WEDNESDAY, August 9th

J.W.King, 3rd Class, a returning Newfoundland soldier, who came aboard at Liverpool in a very weak condition; died at 6.10 a.m. 10.00 a.m. the remains of J.W.King were committed to the deep, the usual rites being performed.[62]

The SS Neptune *carrying troops to join convoy, February 6, 1916*

St. John's on July 19, 1916, bound for England on the SS *Sicilian* and was back on the same vessel for a return voyage home on August 4. Three more men succumbed to the ravages of the Spanish flu, late in 1918. Leonard Hynes, Charles McCarthy, and John Boutcher all died in October 1918 while crossing on the same ship on which a flu epidemic had broken out. More soldiers from the Canadian Expeditionary Force on the same vessel also perished.

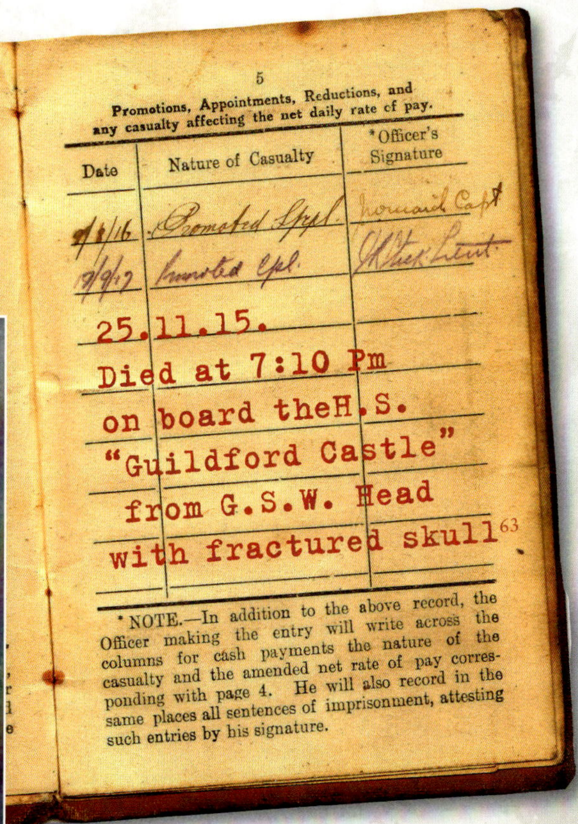

4

For use in case the Rates of Pay given on p. 3 require to be amended—

(1)

The Net Rate of Pay for issue has been reduced or raised to_____ s._____ d. (words)

_____ 191 . on account from_____

5

Promotions, Appointments, Reductions, and any casualty affecting the net daily rate of pay.

Date	Nature of Casualty	*Officer's Signature
9/1/16	Promoted L/Cpl.	[illegible] Capt
1/9/17	Promoted Cpl.	[illegible] Lieut.

25.11.15.
Died at 7:10 Pm
on board the H.S.
"Guildford Castle"
from G.S.W. Head
with fractured skull[63]

*NOTE.—In addition to the above record, the Officer making the entry will write across the columns for cash payments the nature of the casualty and the amended net rate of pay corresponding with page 4. He will also record in the same places all sentences of imprisonment, attesting such entries by his signature.

Frederick Charles Somerton

John Hardy

Commemoration

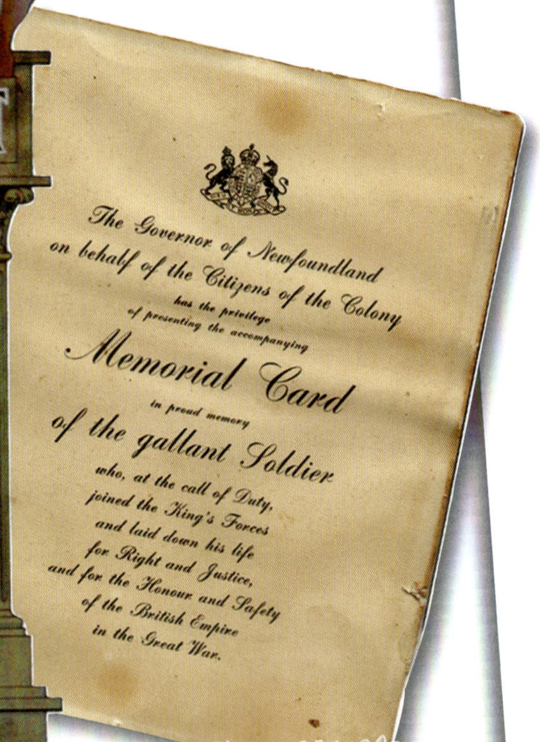
The Governor of Newfoundland
on behalf of the Citizens of the Colony
has the privilege
of presenting the accompanying
Memorial Card
in proud memory
of the gallant Soldier
who, at the call of Duty,
joined the King's Forces
and laid down his life
for Right and Justice,
and for the Honour and Safety
of the British Empire
in the Great War.

Commemorative scrolls issued by the Newfoundland Government to the families of fallen soldiers

In defense unyielding
In attack unflinching
Steady-Unto-Death

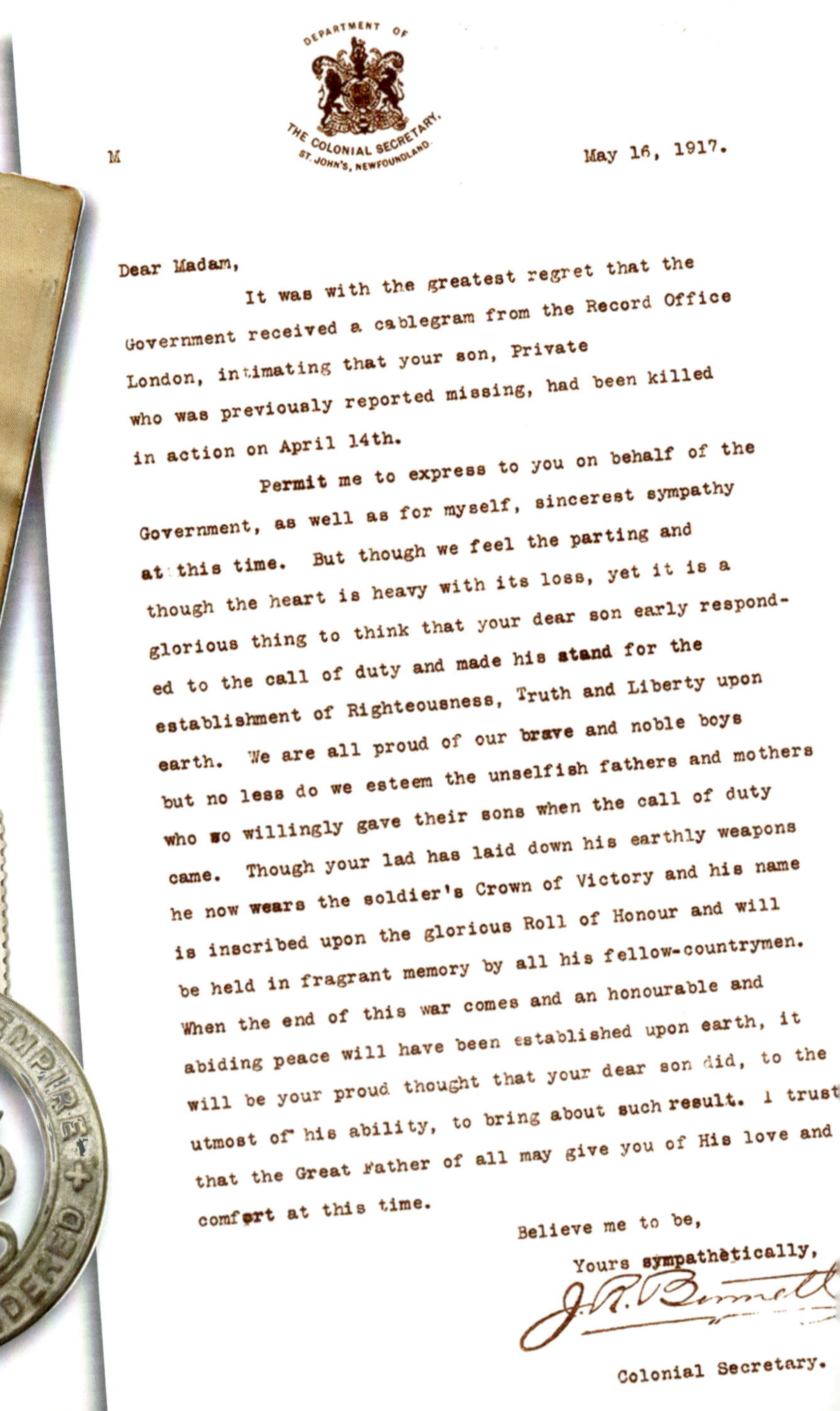
DEPARTMENT OF THE COLONIAL SECRETARY, ST. JOHN'S, NEWFOUNDLAND.

M

May 16, 1917.

Dear Madam,

It was with the greatest regret that the Government received a cablegram from the Record Office London, intimating that your son, Private who was previously reported missing, had been killed in action on April 14th.

Permit me to express to you on behalf of the Government, as well as for myself, sincerest sympathy at this time. But though we feel the parting and though the heart is heavy with its loss, yet it is a glorious thing to think that your dear son early responded to the call of duty and made his stand for the establishment of Righteousness, Truth and Liberty upon earth. We are all proud of our brave and noble boys but no less do we esteem the unselfish fathers and mothers who so willingly gave their sons when the call of duty came. Though your lad has laid down his earthly weapons he now wears the soldier's Crown of Victory and his name is inscribed upon the glorious Roll of Honour and will be held in fragrant memory by all his fellow-countrymen. When the end of this war comes and an honourable and abiding peace will have been established upon earth, it will be your proud thought that your dear son did, to the utmost of his ability, to bring about such result. I trust that the Great Father of all may give you of His love and comfort at this time.

Believe me to be,

Yours sympathetically,

J. R. Bennett

Colonial Secretary.

The Dead Man's Penny

The Dead Man's Penny began as the result of the British government's realization that an official token of gratitude was needed to recognize the service of the fallen. The penny was awarded to the men's next of kin and bereaved families.

At the outset of the war, the government did not expect such high numbers of casualties, and it would become apparent only later that the Commonwealth would suffer such staggering losses. The nation of Newfoundland would become one of the bearers of this loss, and it was not uncommon for a family to be given one of these tokens as recognition of their family member's sacrifice.

Measuring 12 cm in diameter the disk was made from cast gun metal and incorporated the design of the symbolic English lion along with the figure of Britannia. The name of the fallen soldier would be inscribed in the rectangular area along with a second lion at the very bottom tearing Imperial Germany's eagle to pieces. At the flanks, dolphins swim, representing British naval dominance, and an inscription reads "He Died for Freedom and Honour."

One such family from Newfoundland that received the Dead Man's Penny was that of Captain James Allan Ledingham. It would be a story all too familiar to other families across the country. As the war left a wake of grief in the communities throughout the various towns, often the Dead Man's Penny was the only closure a family would receive. Ledingham's remains were never identified and the only token of his sacrifice from the British would be this circular medallion.

James Allan Ledingham was killed in action at Broembeek River, October 9, 1917. He commanded "A" Company at the Battle of Poelcapelle.

Ledingham was later commemorated on the Tablets in Newfoundland Memorial Park and has No Known Grave.

Alex Ledingham

Agnes Allan Ledingham (Mrs. Templeton)

"Survivors are full of stories of the courage of their comrades. They tell how Captain A. J. Ledingham, [sic] the youngest captain, led his company in charge; how he fell wounded in three places; how he crawled into a shell hole and lay there more dead than alive for upwards of five hours. Then he heard the moaning of a comrade, and peeping over the edge of his shelter saw lying a few yards away his old Newfoundland chum Lieutenant Robertson, almost at his last gasp. Captain Ledingham, hardly able to move crawled to his comrade, and there, under rain of shot and shell, hoisted the Lieutenant on his back and crawled with him to the British lines."[64]

"He is not dead - my friend, there is no death,
His strong and tireless soul
Marches to some great goal!"[65]

May 25th, 1916

My Dear Agnes,

You will at once say it's about time I thought of addressing you and wonder what kind of brother I am, but as you know, there is very little I can write about, things military being taboo, and as that occupies all our time and thoughts, it leaves nothing to hold forth on ....

... I hear from Alex often. His letters only take one day to reach me, so you see he is not so very far away. The odd part of it is that although I know what part of the line he is in, he doesn't know where I am. I am unable to let him know- but expect he will eventually find out. I am glad he succeeded in getting his commission and feel certain that he has deserved it after coming through the ranks ....

... If it weren't for this trench, life would be fairly tolerable. This has its funny sides as well as its sad ones. Here's one of the funny bits. A few nights ago, I was crawling about in front of our line in " no mans land", that's the bit between us and the Bosche. I was quite near their line and I could hear them working with barbed wire, driving stakes, etc. and distincly heard one who was hammering something, whistling the following tune "many brave hearts are asleep in the deep". I wonder if he was thinking of our navy or German submarines. Another one of our men heard someone playing "on the Mississippi" on a tin whistle.

Hope you are keeping well and that you are having decent weather. I very nearly forgot the chief object of this letter, which was to wish you many happy returns of the 18th of May. Hope to be with you all before the next and express the wishes personally.

With love to Anna Catherine Robert, Arthur and self.
Your loving brother, Jim[66]

Padre Thomas Nangle

The erection of the five Newfoundland memorial parks in France and Belgium, and the National War Memorial in St. John's, were primarily the work of the Rev. Thomas Nangle, the tireless Regiment Padre who stayed on after the war to make sure Newfoundland's fallen heroes were properly commemorated. Thanks to Nangle, people in Newfoundland and Labrador have memorials to be proud of. He spent many hours overseeing re-interment parties, searched for the missing, negotiated prices, photographed burials and cemeteries, compiled lists of the missing, and negotiated with landowners and government commissions for suitable locations for Newfoundland's memorials. In 1919 he identified the locations of the current sites as desirable for Newfoundland, and such was his persuasive manner that he was successful in all his endeavours save for one. As late as 1922 it was clearly Nangle's intention to have the Memorial Bronze Tablets placed at the National War Memorial in St. John's. He went so far as to ask Sir Richard Squires, Prime Minister of Newfoundland, to instruct the Imperial War Graves Commission (forerunners of the Commonwealth War Graves Commission) to that effect.

For reasons yet unknown, but which may have had something to do with the funds contributed to the project by the IWGC, these tablets were placed far from home at Beaumont-Hamel, France. The names of these men were finally repatriated in July 2009.

Unveiling of The Caribou, Newfoundland Memorial Park, 1925

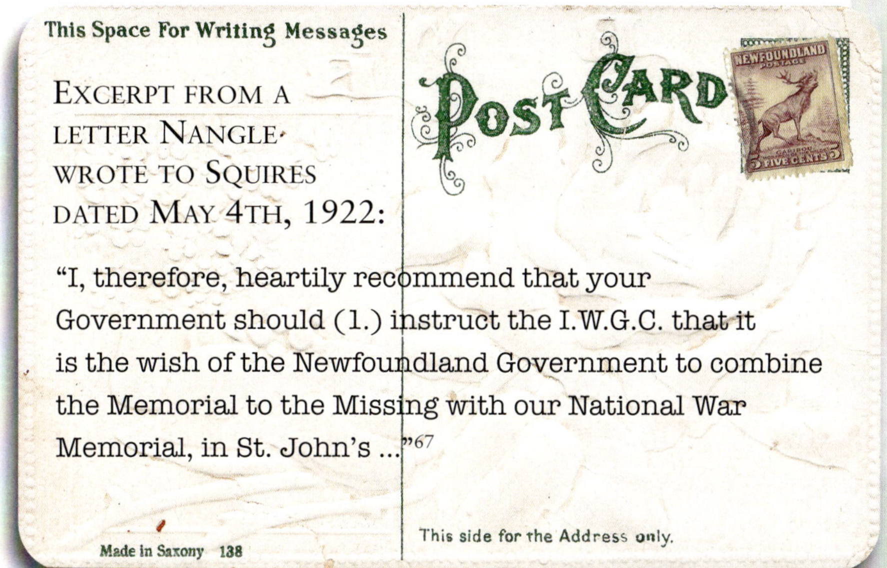

Excerpt from a letter Nangle wrote to Squires dated May 4th, 1922:

"I, therefore, heartily recommend that your Government should (1.) instruct the I.W.G.C. that it is the wish of the Newfoundland Government to combine the Memorial to the Missing with our National War Memorial, in St. John's ..."[67]

Souvenir
OF
First Memorial Flight
OVER
St. John's and Vicinity
In connection with
Newfoundland War Memorial Campaign
February 1922.

Curlers' Memorial Day
FEBRUARY 15TH. 1922
Through the courtesy of Major Cotton and Captain Bennett, this entitles bearer to one flight in the Martinsyde Aeroplane.
President.
Secretary-Treasurer.
PILOT Major.
ASS'T PILOT Captain.
PADRE NANGLE
(Date) FEBRUARY, 1922

CAPTAIN G. WHITTY, O.B.E., M.C. PHOTO ALBUM.
COURTESY OF CAROLINE BALL

Nangle with Field Marshall Haig June 7, 1925

Newfoundland Memorial Park
Beaumont-Hamel, France

Newfoundland Memorial Park was officially opened by Earl Haig on June 7, 1925. Haig was the supreme commander of the British Expeditionary Force during most of the war. The Newfoundland Government had secured surplus war guns to place in various locations around the park, and according to Capt. G. Whitty, close friend to Thomas Nangle, Nangle's original vision was to recreate the battlefield, with restored trenches and guns giving visitors a graphic reproduction of the actual battle that day.

"In years to come much more costly memorials of greater architectural and sculptural beauty may be erected by the nations but none will be more unique or appealing to future generations than the simple tribute made by Newfoundland to her gallant sons…"[68]

Today the park is remarkably serene, the guns are gone, and the grass has overtaken the trenches and shell-holes, yet the effect is no less today than what Nangle wanted all visitors to feel when walking through the park. Nangle negotiated with as many as 250 landowners to purchase the grounds for the park and the cost was borne mostly by the Newfoundland Government who paid $40,000, with another $8815.00 raised through public subscription.

FRENCH AND BRITTISH SOLDIERS,
NEWFOUNDLAND PARK COMMEMORATION JUNE 7, 1925

The Danger Tree

For many who survived that fateful morning on July 1, the Danger Tree, the lone reference point on a battle-scarred ground, garnered a place of reverence. Located roughly halfway between German and British front lines, it was one of two areas where, prior to the battle, the wire had been cut for the Newfoundlanders to pass through. It was the forming up place during the two trench raids in the days leading up to the battle, and was the area from which the Newfoundlanders moved forward in search of wounded comrades on the night of the second raid. More than 80 Newfoundland men were cut to pieces near this tree on July 1. This tree stands as a natural monument to the fallen of the Newfoundland Regiment on July 1, 1916, and is considered just as important a memorial to Newfoundland's fallen as the Caribou and the park itself.

The Danger Tree, Beaumont-Hamel, January 2009

The Danger Tree prior to 1923

> "THEN PICKING OUR WAY OVER TRENCHES AND BARBED WIRE, PASSING THE PLACE WHERE 'DANGER TREE' ONCE STOOD (NOW RE-ERECTED) IN NO-MAN'S-LAND ON THE EDGE OF ONE OF THOSE HAWTHORN RIDGES ..." – R.H. Cochius April 1924[69]

The oldest photo taken shows how much of an advantage the Germans had. The men silhouetted against the skyline made easy targets for machine gunners. The background on this page is possibly the same tree cut, trimmed, and set into the ground by Cochius and was taken around the time the park was opened in the 1920s. The newest photograph was taken by the authors in January 2009 and shows the replica, the original tree having been replaced sometime after World War II.

THE DANGER TREE, BEAUMONT-HAMEL, C. 1923

Rudolph Cochius

Rudolph Cochius

R.H.K. Cochius was born, raised, and educated in Holland. He first came to Newfoundland in the employ of Sir Edgar Bowring in 1912, who commissioned him to design and construct Bowring Park in the west end of St. John's, beginning a 25-year relationship between Newfoundland and this talented landscape architect. In 1922 he was contracted to design and build the five battlefield memorials in France and Belgium dedicated to the brave soldiers of Newfoundland. Working closely with Father Nangle, and taking cues from his vision, Cochius gave Newfoundland five memorial parks to forever commemorate her gallant sons.

In the company of Father Nangle during his first visit to the proposed battlefield memorial sites, Cochius was deeply moved. "Back again in my quiet peaceful Dutch town a few days later, after having been rushed through so much desolation, to me it all seemed a dream – or was it a nightmare!"[70] Though Newfoundland could not match the millions of dollars pouring into other national monuments like Delville Wood (South Africa) and Vimy Ridge (Canada), Cochius was adamant that Beaumont-Hamel would be the crowning achievement of all battlefield memorials. He believed that the vehement outcry of the mourning caribou placed in the "... heart of one gigantic graveyard"[71] overlooking the battle-scarred ground would emerge as a destination of pilgrimage for people of many nations, not just Newfoundland.

View from log cabin

Old log cabin Visitors Centre

"... FOR THOSE WHO HOLD THIS COUNTRY DEAR AND WHO ARE PROUD OF ITS SONS OF THE NEWFOUNDLAND REGIMENT I FELT TOO THAT THE SPOT SHOULD BE PRESERVED IN ITS WAR-TIME-STATE, WITH ITS TRENCHES, ITS NO-MAN'S-LAND, ITS DUG-OUTS, AS A PERPETUAL REMINDER FOR FUTURE GENERATIONS AS A SACRED GROUND."[72]

Cochius delivered Nangle's vision, and to this day the Newfoundland Memorial Park attracts hundreds of thousands of visitors each year. It has become as Cochius had envisioned, a place of pilgrimage that ranks alongside Menin Gate, Delville Wood, Theipval, and Vimy Ridge.

JOHN OXENHAM POEM NEAR PARK ENTRANCE

William "Bill" Brown

William Brown was the first curator of the Newfoundland Memorial Park and held that position from 1924 to 1954, the year he died from a massive heart attack at the park's entrance. He married a woman from Auchonvillers and is buried with a simple headstone marked William Brown of Newfoundland. Brown, however, had never set foot in Newfoundland; he was born in Grimsby, England, and served as a lorry driver with the Canadian Army during the war. He came into the employ of Father Thomas Nangle in 1920 after being discharged. He lived on site, but according to some, had a house he refused to sleep in, and requested not to be buried in his wife's family plot. He assisted Father Nangle in the work of exhuming, identifying and reburying Newfoundland's dead across the battlefields of France and Belgium. He was recommended by Father Nangle for the Order of the British Empire, along with James Lambert and John Lawrence Murphy, for their tireless and gruesome task of re-interring Newfoundland's war dead. Along with Nangle's, their contributions failed to garner any official recognition.

William Brown's Headstone Auchonvillers Communal Cemetery, near Beaumont-Hamel, France

Perhaps traumatised by the horrors of war and its aftermath, he could no longer face the peacefulness of home and never abandoned his comrades, except when Brown fled to England during the Second World War with his wife and child. He promptly returned after and was back on the job by 1945. He sent pictures to the Newfoundland Government showing the state of disrepair. Today his gravesite sits alone in the Auchonvillers Communal Cemetery just down the road from the park he so lovingly cared for.

The photo on the right is the remains of an unknown British soldier being escorted through Bolougne, France, on November 8, 1920, destined for Westminster Abbey to be buried among kings. The coffin was made of oak from Hampton Court, and a sixteenth-century crusader's sword from the king's collection was placed within the wrought-iron bands that bound the coffin. The coffin was placed in its current resting place on November 11, 1920, and was closed on November 18.

Homecoming of the Unknown Warrior Marshall Foch saluting the body on the outskirts of Boulogne

"The body of the Unknown Warrior may be from any of the three services, Army, Navy or Air Force, and from any part of the British Isles, Dominions or Colonies and represents all those who have no other memorial."[73]

One of the men escorting the Unknown Warrior was Sergeant Major Bill Brown, supposedly of the Royal Newfoundland Regiment, who worked with Padre Nangle on reburying Newfoundland's dead, and was the first caretaker of the Newfoundland War Memorial Park in Beaumont-Hamel.

EVOLUTION OF THE CARIBOU

Postcard by S. H. Parsons taken around the turn of the century

CAPTAIN G. WHITTY, O.B.E., M.C. PHOTO ALBUM.
COURTESY OF CAROLINE BALL

Possibly a casting from the maquette used to create full-sized Caribou

CAPTAIN G. WHITTY, O.B.E., M.C. PHOTO ALBUM.
COURTESY OF CAROLINE BALL

Installation of the Caribou, Beaumont-Hamel

CAPTAIN G. WHITTY, O.B.E., M.C. PHOTO ALBUM.
COURTESY OF CAROLINE BALL

Newfoundland Memorial Park before placement of the Caribou

CAPTAIN G. WHITTY, O.B.E., M.C.
PHOTO ALBUM.
COURTESY OF CAROLINE BALL

Rudolph Cochius, Architect of Bowring Park and Newfoundland Memorial Park

The Lost Nation

People often wonder, without fully understanding, why a single regiment has five battlefield memorials in France and Belgium. These are not just Regiment memorials, but national memorials. They are there to commemorate Newfoundland's commitment to the war. The fact that the tiny nation could raise and sustain only one battalion has no bearing on the sacrifices she made, and like other nations, Newfoundland wanted to remember her fallen with dignity. When you walk into the Newfoundland Memorial Park in Beaumont-Hamel the first monument you see is the 29th Division Memorial. The 1st Battalion, Royal Newfoundland Regiment, was one of twelve infantry battalions that made up the Division, and it is a testament to the stalwart bravery of Newfoundland's men that the Division chose to place its memorial inside Newfoundland's national battlefield memorial. The 51st Highland Division also has its memorial located inside the park, commemorating its part in the closing days of the Battle of the Somme when that Division launched a successful assault on Beaumont-Hamel in November 1916.

The heavy toll Newfoundland incurred from the Great War eventually led to its financial and patriotic collapse. By 1933, struggling to make interest payments on loans taken out to purchase the Reid Newfoundland Railway, fund veterans' pensions, and participate in the war, coupled with the worldwide Great Depression, Newfoundland was "gently" persuaded by the British to relinquish her democratic right and aspirations of nationhood. The war had been instrumental in building the nations of Canada, Australia, and New Zealand, but in Newfoundland's case, despite the patriotic fervour of the returning soldiers (many of whom left the country in 1920-21 during disastrous fishery reforms), the war would be her ultimate downfall. Many of the men who would have been counted on to lead the country into the next phase lay buried in France, and those who survived returned to a political environment and economy that made no room for them. July 1, 1916, was devastating on so many levels. Newfoundland's brightest and best were slaughtered. Brave men continued marching into oblivion as the war raged on. Without these men, with fresh ideas and a patriotic élan to combat the "merchant of Water Street," Newfoundland's days of independence would draw to a close.

John Shiwak in an unofficial studio uniform

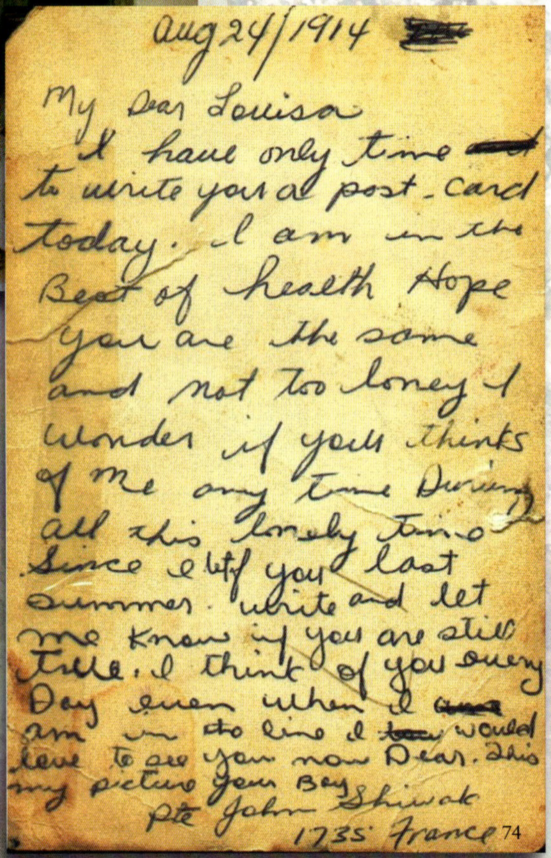

Aug 24/1914

My Dear Louisa
I have only time to write you a post-card today. I am in the Best of health Hope you are the same and not too loney I wonder if you thinks of me any time During all this lonely time Since I left you last summer. write and let me know if you are still tille. I think of you every Day even when I am in the line I would love to see you now Dear. this my picture your Boy
Pte John Shiwak
1735 France 74

Labrador

There are four men on the tablets who came from Labrador. The three from the Royal Newfoundland Regiment, John Shiwak , Charles Mesher, and Daniel Groves, all hailed from Rigolet. Their Regiment numbers also suggest that they signed up together. A fourth, John James of Forteau, died while serving on the HM trawler *Vivanti* as a member of the Newfoundland Royal Naval Reserve when she foundered off Hastings on March 7, 1917.

John Shiwak was an accomplished Inuit hunter and trapper who put his skills to good use in the Newfoundland Regiment. Known to be one of the best snipers in the British Army, he was loved by all ranks. It was said that he had a lot of "notches" on his gun and that sniping was a lot like "swatching," a sealer's term for hunting seals as they poke their heads up for air in holes in the ice. He was also known as a gifted writer and artist. When his two friends and fellow trappers Charles Mesher and Daniel Groves were killed at Monchy-le-Preux, Shiwak went into a deep depression. He could not understand the senseless loss of life. The day after the Battle of Cambrai was launched, Shiwak was killed from a direct artillery hit, along with others, as the Regiment walked along the canal bank in Masnieres.

57. B. C26. B. 9. 5 (REF.NO. 813W)

Captain R.H. Tait in a Letter written to Dr. Padden's sister wrote:

"...We assembled in the ('Sucrerie') and, having formed up, proceeded along the (canal bank) towards another sugar factory ... The enemy were at the time shelling the bank, and one shell burst right in the middle of our column and killed seven, amongst whom was L/C Shiwak ... Shiwak was buried that afternoon in the village of Masnieres and close to the spot where he fell ... His loss was keenly felt by the whole Regiment, as he was a great favourite with all ranks, an excellent scout and observer and a thoroughly good and reliable fellow in everyway. Shiwak will long be remembered by all who knew him."[75]

Charles Mesher's Memorial, Port Blandford

The sister ship of HM Trawler Vivanti

John James

Daniel Groves

George Taylor

Eugene Taylor

Richard Taylor

FAMILIES

Only a mother can tell you of the sorrow of answering the door, with the local priest or minister on the other side clutching a telegram. His job was to ease the news and provide immediate comfort and solace to the bereaved mother. Worse still is the second visit, or in the case of Mary Taylor of the Battery Road in St. John's, two visits, and three sons. One can only imagine her anguish as the minister informed her that both Richard and Eugene died and were missing at the Battle of Monchy-le-Preux, nine months after losing George at Beaumont-Hamel. It is hard to put yourself in her place: not only has she lost three dear sons, but none has had a proper burial. All three occupy places on the Regiment Tablet at Beaumont-Hamel for those with no known graves. There is no comfort one can give for such a tragedy. Yet Mary was not the only mother to have lost more than one son; quite a few families in Newfoundland and elsewhere lost two sons who fought for the Regiment or drowned as members of the Newfoundland Mercantile Marine or Newfoundland Royal Naval Reserve.

Stanley & George Abbott

TROIS ARBES

The tablets contain sixteen known sets of brothers. Many of them reside in perpetuity on the tablets side by each, as they did growing up in Newfoundland. George and Stanley Abbott of Battery Road in St. John's are commemorated alongside one another as they died within minutes at Beaumont-Hamel on July 1. Other brothers who died in the same engagement include Hector and William Bennett of Stephenville, died and missing at Monchy-le-Preux, April 14, 1917, John Roy and Stewart Small Ferguson, officers lost at Beaumont-Hamel. Newfoundland

Royal Naval Reservists George and Thomas Youden of Bull's Cove (Georgetown, Brigus) went down on the HMS *Viknor* on January 13, 1915.

Other identified sibling losses with no known graves from the Royal Newfoundland Regiment are Esau and George Baker of Clarenville, George and Walter Clarke of Springdale, John Joseph and Edmond Dunphy of St. John's, Cyril and Edward James Gardner of British Harbour, Aaron and William John King of Bonaventure, Herbert and John Moulton of Burin, Leaton and Robert Ronald Simms of St. Anthony, Hugh and Alexander Williams of Springdale, and Leo Michael and Richard Patrick Voisey of St. John's. Frederick and John Thomas Morgan, two brothers from Seal Cove, Conception Bay, and Harold and George Coates of Fogo, died while serving the Newfoundland Royal Naval Reserve.

Besides the brothers commemorated together on the tablets, there are more who are divided in death, one on the tablet, the other in the ground with a headstone. One notable pair are George and Charles Chuck of Russia. George is memorialized on the tablet, while brother Charles lies alone in the Chapel's Cove Cemetery, a victim of his wounds and the Spanish flu. George Lukins died at Beaumont-Hamel days after his brother Jack was killed in a trench raid. George is buried in the Hawthorne Ridge No. 2 Cemetery; Jack is on the tablet. On the Newfoundland Mercantile Marine Tablet are numerous relatives, including fathers and sons, uncles and cousins. Such is the nature of shipping in Newfoundland that many of the schooners plying the trade were family-run businesses. Though it is much harder to identify relatives in these cases, it is known that Captain Andrew Wilson Senior asked his son to accompany him on the ill-fated transatlantic voyage of the SS *Beverly*. Another father and son duo were Isaac and Mac Bartlett of Bell Island, who were lost on the schooner *L.H.B.* when it was sunk by a German submarine en route to Gibraltar in October 1916. Isaac was an old man but had his captain's papers and accompanied his son Mac overseas. Mac's family believed that the day he died there was a tap on his Aunt Ann Andrews' kitchen window (a habit of Mac's) to signify that he was visiting, but when they went to the door he was nowhere to be found. Isaac's wife Sarah had lost another son, John Dawe Bartlett, in 1901 at the age of 21.

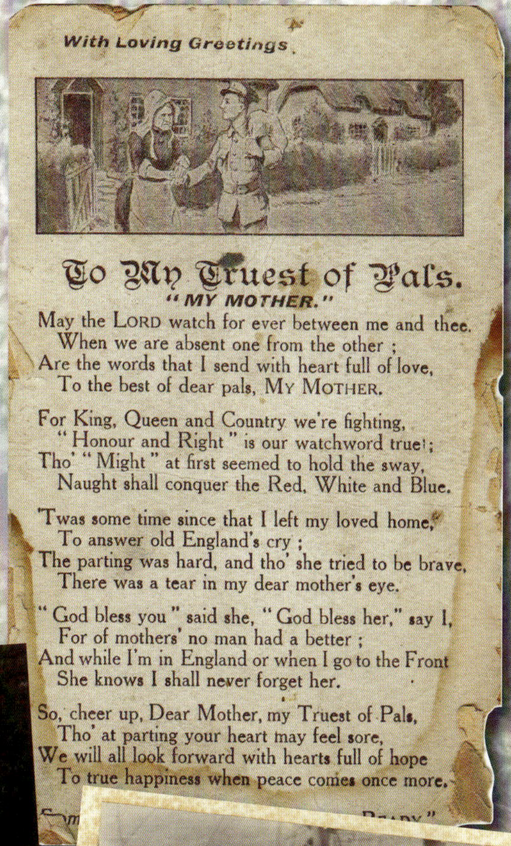

With Loving Greetings.

To My Truest of Pals.

"MY MOTHER."

May the LORD watch for ever between me and thee.
When we are absent one from the other ;
Are the words that I send with heart full of love,
To the best of dear pals, MY MOTHER.

For King, Queen and Country we're fighting,
"Honour and Right" is our watchword true!;
Tho' "Might" at first seemed to hold the sway,
Naught shall conquer the Red, White and Blue.

'Twas some time since that I left my loved home,
To answer old England's cry ;
The parting was hard, and tho' she tried to be brave,
There was a tear in my dear mother's eye.

"God bless you" said she, "God bless her," say I,
For of mothers' no man had a better ;
And while I'm in England or when I go to the Front
She knows I shall never forget her.

So, cheer up, Dear Mother, my Truest of Pals,
Tho' at parting your heart may feel sore,
We will all look forward with hearts full of hope
To true happiness when peace comes once more.

Edward James Gardner, brother of Cyril Gardner

George & Harold Coates

No Known Graves

329 PRIVATE
L. HOLDEN
ROYAL NEWFOUNDLAND REGT.
1ST JULY 1916, AGE 21

THERE ARE 592 NAMES INSCRIBED ON THE ROYAL NEWFOUNDLAND MEMORIAL TABLET, BUT NOT ALL NAMES CONTAINED ON THE TABLET ARE ACTUALLY MISSING WITH NO KNOWN GRAVES.

Five men on the tablet have headstones; four are located in Serre Cemetery No. 2, and one is located at Longueval. The four men located at Serre are Arthur Driscoll, Lucas Holden, Martin Farrell, and George Winsor. The other man, Michael Cahill, is buried at Longueval, Somme, far from the attack on July 1. One other name is inscribed on the tablet that is commemorated elsewhere; 2nd Lt. Harold George Barrett of St. John's is also remembered on the Tyne Cot Memorial in Belgium. He was killed at the Battle of Langemarck (Steenbeek) on August 16, 1917. Another man, Solomon Clarke, a merchant mariner, may also be buried in the Old Salvation Army Cemetery in Carbonear.

H. G. Barrett

Gerald Ayre

Richard Pitman

Foreign Nationals

It is often forgotten that the tablets are in remembrance to those who served with Newfoundland forces during the war and have no known graves. Many erroneously write that they are native Newfoundlanders or Labradorians only. But this is not the case; there are a number of identified foreign nationals on the tablets and many others who served in the Regiment. On the Newfoundland Mercantile Marine Tablet there are four men commemorated from foreign lands. There is a John Brest from Lunenberg, Nova Scotia, who perished on the SS *Watagua* when it was sunk in the mid-Atlantic by a German U-boat. As well, Arthur Licence of Stoke, Ipswich, England; Jose Torres of Chancho, Chile; and John Stewart of Drogheda, Ireland, were lost on the schooner *M.C. McKay* out of Twillingate.

THE NEWFOUNDLAND FORCES COMPRISED MORE THAN NATIVE NEWFOUNDLANDERS.

There are a number of foreigners as well who served with the Royal Newfoundland Regiment. George Chuck was born in a small village 150 miles east of Petrograd, Russia, and with his brother Charles, immigrated to Newfoundland in 1913 to work as miners on Bell Island. Both joined the Newfoundland Regiment even though they were foreign nationals and could barely speak English. A magistrate on Bell Island had to vouch for their integrity before they were allowed to join. Charles married a woman from Harbour Main, Maggie Barron, shortly before he

Grave of Charles Chuck, brother of George Chuck, located in Chapel's Cove, Newfoundland George is commemorated on his brother's headstone.

In loving Memory
of no 2496 Pte Charles
Chuck
Beloved husband of
Margaret Chuck
Who Died at Hr Main
Jan 16, 1919
While in the service of
King and Country
Aged 27 years
May His soul rest
in peace

Erected by his beloved
wife

Also his beloved
brother
no. 2497. pte
George chuck
killed in the battle
of monchy
april 14 1917 aged 24 yrs
may the lord have
mercy on their souls

enlisted. Parents of the brothers were dead and Maggie became their sole family. George was killed and subsequently missing at Monchy-le-Preux, leaving all his property to Maggie. Charles, Maggie's husband, was wounded at Bailleul, April 10, 1918, arrived in St. John's December 21, 1918, contracted the Spanish flu, and died January 16, 1919, at Lakeview, Harbour Main, before he was demobilised. Today his headstone sits quietly in the Chapel's Cove Cemetery with a memorial to his brother at its base. Maggie buried her husband in her father's plot and paid for the headstone even though it should have been the responsibility of the IWGC to pay and bury Charles in accordance with their guidelines. These two brothers fought for a foreign country in a faraway land against a common enemy and paid the supreme sacrifice in service to their adopted homeland.

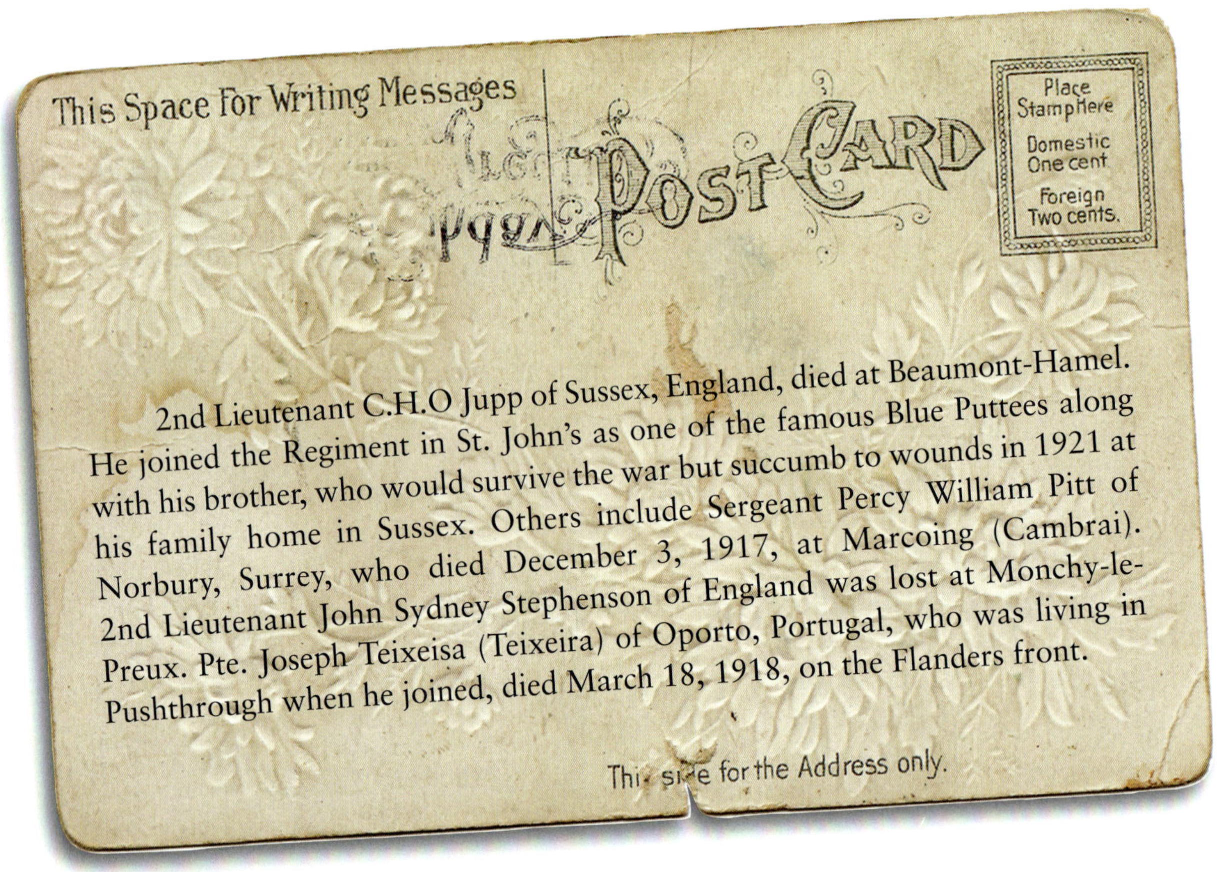

2nd Lieutenant C.H.O Jupp of Sussex, England, died at Beaumont-Hamel. He joined the Regiment in St. John's as one of the famous Blue Puttees along with his brother, who would survive the war but succumb to wounds in 1921 at his family home in Sussex. Others include Sergeant Percy William Pitt of Norbury, Surrey, who died December 3, 1917, at Marcoing (Cambrai). 2nd Lieutenant John Sydney Stephenson of England was lost at Monchy-le-Preux. Pte. Joseph Teixeisa (Teixeira) of Oporto, Portugal, who was living in Pushthrough when he joined, died March 18, 1918, on the Flanders front.

John Booth of Peterhead, Scotland, # 2405, Age 27, Died at Broembeek.

Biographies

Douglas Haig

CAPTAIN G. WHITTY, O.B.E., M.C. PHOTO ALBUM. COURTESY OF CAROLINE BALL

Sir Douglas Haig was a cavalry man. A career soldier, he saw action in Egypt during the Sudan Campaign in 1898 and in South Africa from 1899-1902. First promoted to General in 1914, he took command of I Corps and a short time later took command of the First Army. In 1915 he succeeded General John French as Commander-in-Chief of the British Expeditionary Force in France, a position he held until 1919. He was made Field Marshall by King George V in January 1917. Loathed and loved, Haig is a controversial figure to this day. After the war he formed a close relationship with Father Thomas Nangle and was invited by Nangle to open the Newfoundland National War Memorial in St. John's in 1924 and the Newfoundland Memorial Park in Beaumont-Hamel, France, in 1925.

Sydney Frost

Nova Scotian, Captain Sydney Frost was a Bank of Nova Scotia employee in St. John's when he enlisted in the Newfoundland Regiment in 1914. He was one of the few Blue Puttees who saw action throughout the war. As part of the 10% reserve at Beaumont-Hamel he was thrown into the line on the afternoon of July 1, where he was instrumental in bringing in three wounded soldiers. Four months later he was wounded at Gueudecourt. He won the Military Cross in 1918 while " … He led his company with dash and kept battalion headquarters well informed as to the situation. When the advance was held up at Keiberg Ridge by a 6-in. gun and two machine guns, he pushed his Lewis guns out to either flank, and made a direct attack by short rushes with a platoon capturing the gun and both machine guns. His prompt action led to the capture of the ridge."[76] He spent his lifetime remembering his fallen comrades, even undertaking the enormous task in the early sixties of visiting and photographing all the Regiment graves in Belgium, France, England, Malta, Egypt, and Gallipoli when he retired from the Bank of Nova Scotia as President. He provided much material to G.W.L. Nicholson's sprawling history *The Fighting Newfoundlander*. He played a role in compiling the list for *The Newfoundland Book of Remembrance* in the late sixties and early seventies. He kept large scrapbooks on the Regiment that had newspaper clippings and photos over many years. He returned to Beaumont-Hamel in 1961 as the highest ranking veteran when the park unveiled the new superintendent's house and a new commemorative plaque.

Arthur Hadow

Arthur Hadow and James Forbes-Robertson

CAPTAIN G. WHITTY, O.B.E., M.C. PHOTO ALBUM. COURTESY OF CAROLINE BALL

Lt.-Colonel Arthur Hadow was made commanding officer of the 1st Battalion in December 1915. A career soldier, Hadow had spent most of his duty in South Africa, India, Tibet, and Egypt prior to the outbreak of war. Known as a task master and disciplinarian, he initially did not garner much respect from the men, though the officers seemed to adore him. He is credited with turning a rag-tag bunch of volunteer "colonials" into a crack fighting unit within the professional 29th Division. He was in command of the Regiment at Beaumont-Hamel when the wounded soldiers returned to the trenches asking "Is the Colonel pleased?" He relinquished command of the Newfoundlanders in late 1917.

James Forbes-Robertson

James Forbes-Robertson, like Hadow, is credited with having been one of the motivating forces in turning the Newfoundland Regiment into a professional fighting unit. He was a career British officer. While acting commander of the Regiment at Monchy-le-Preux, he cobbled together a handful of men to defend the village from a German counterattack. He was awarded the Military Cross on January 1, 1917, for distinguished service in the field. He was awarded the Distinguished Service Order for conspicuous gallantry at Monchy-le-Preux. He was awarded the Victoria Cross while serving the Border Regiment in 1918. *London Gazette*: "By his magnificent example on four separate occasions he saved the line from breaking. When troops in front were falling back, he made a rapid reconnaissance on horseback, in full view of the enemy, under heavy machine-gun fire and close-range shell fire. He then organized and, still mounted, led a counter attack which was completely successful in re-establishing our line. When his horse was shot from under him he continued on foot. His horse was wounded three times and he was thrown five times."[77]

CAPTAIN G. WHITTY, O.B.E., M.C. PHOTO ALBUM. COURTESY OF CAROLINE BALL

Gerald Whitty

Captain Gerald Whitty, OBE, MC, a great Newfoundland patriot, was instrumental in raising money for the National War Memorial, and was a close friend and confidant of Padre Nangle. He saw action in Gallipoli and led a heroic charge at Masnieres on November 20, 1917, in which he was wounded and later won the Military Cross. After the war he became the secretary-treasurer of the Great War Veterans Association, played a prominent role in raising funds for the National War Memorial in St. John's, and organized the ceremonies around the unveiling of the memorial and the visit of Field Marshall Douglas Haig. He was killed by a speeding driver in September 1924 while waiting to board a bus to return to St. John's after having dinner in Donovans. The driver killed six people in the accident, and spent one year in jail for manslaughter.

Walter Davidson

Sir Walter Davidson was appointed the Governor of Newfoundland in 1913, at a time of heightened prosperity. He held positions previously in Ceylon (Sri Lanka) and Transvaal, and spent eight years as the Governor of the Seychelles Islands before coming to Newfoundland. Davidson played an integral role in Newfoundland's war effort, especially in the areas of recruitment and promotions. He was chairman of the Newfoundland Patriotic Association and dabbled in the public affairs of the country more so than some of his predecessors, which caused a great deal of tension. He was reassigned to New South Wales in 1917, after Newfoundland's war effort began running into recruitment trouble.

Gerald W.L. Nicholson

Colonel Gerald W.L. Nicholson, career soldier and official historian of the Canadian Army, worked for the Historical Section of the Canadian Military until his retirement in 1961. He was contracted by Newfoundland Premier Joey Smallwood to write the official history of the volunteers who served with Newfoundland forces on land, sea, and air. Spanning almost 200 years, the two large volumes of his work are often cited in publications about the Newfoundland Regiment from 1795 through the early 1960s. He also wrote the history of Newfoundland's contribution in World War II, including the 59th (Newfoundland) Heavy Regiment, 166th (Newfoundland) Field Artillery, Royal Navy, and 125th (Newfoundland) Squadron Royal Air Force. He left behind numerous papers relating to Newfoundland forces that can be accessed through the National Archives of Canada.

The Legacy

The Regiment left Newfoundland and Labrador with a proud military and national heritage, one that should be upheld and remembered. Although there are now two memorials to the missing, we must not forget that these men still lie buried in the fields of France and Belgium. It is sobering to look down the gentle slope, undulating with trenches, craters, and cemeteries, towards the German defensive position in front of the infamous Y-Ravine. With the Danger Tree roughly marking the halfway point through no man's land and the place where many of the men came to rest permanently, only the hardened heart could fail to be moved. Viewing the tablets placed at Bowring Park cannot replace the impact of standing on the hallowed soil of Beaumont-Hamel.

Memorial plaque located in the Notre Dame Cathedral, Paris

French doctors, World War I era postcard.

LA LAITERIE MILITAR

Rebuilt trench behind Avril Williams' Ocean Villas Tea Room, Auchonvillers. This trench was used by the 29th Division (including Newfoundland Regiment) to move to the front lines prior to the Battle of the Somme.

One of the first places the replication team (Morgan MacDonald and Frank Gogos, along with Bob Hood and Randal Power) visited after the Newfoundland Memorial Park was the Ancre British Cemetery located between Hamel and Beaumont-Hamel. It was an eerie feeling to stand among hundreds of graves while the sun crested the opposite ridge. The manicured grass was crisp beneath our feet from the early morning frost, and the frozen dew coated the white headstones with a thin veneer. With camera in hand, I scanned the neat rows of tablets, searching for the caribou insignia that identified the lads who gave their lives on July 1 for Newfoundland and King. While some were identified, more often than not, the caribou carving was followed by “A Soldier of the Great War Royal Newfoundland Regiment,” a single cross, and “Known unto God” inscribed at the base of the stone.

Spending seven days on the Somme, a good many of them in the Newfoundland Memorial Park at Beaumont-Hamel, was a life-changing experience not just for me, but for the entire team. The sheer destruction has been methodically ploughed by returning farmers into neat little fields that belie their true history and the secrets they contain: the missing interred without burial, and unexploded ordnance, much of it as lethal today as it was then. Neat rows of ivory headstones are laid out with architectural precision, populating the manicured grass in the thousands and surrounded by smart stone walls. Hundreds of these Commonwealth graves are scattered throughout the countryside. Some are very difficult to get to, located in the middle of a swampy mud field, and if you’re lucky, a perfect straight green path leads you in. Some cemeteries do not have paths, and yet others have narrow paved lanes that end abruptly at a front gate. When you drive through the back roads of the Somme there is hardly a time when your view does not include the telltale marker of yet another cemetery, the “Cross of Sacrifice” looming over the dead, keeping a silent vigil.

Much of what belonged to the Royal Newfoundland Regiment has been saved and displayed by dedicated volunteers working with a shoestring budget or no budget at all. They need help to preserve and collect the last of the medals, papers, photos, stories and memories. I believe the first step has been undertaken with the repatriation of the names of Newfoundland and Labrador's missing. Now it is up to us to use these replicas to retell the stories of the proud soldiers. Everyone from Newfoundland and Labrador should learn about Beaumont-Hamel and the sacrifices our ancestors made. Hordes of French and British school children can tell you about Beaumont-Hamel and the Battle of the Somme, and many Newfoundlanders and Labradorians cannot. While we worked, buses full of high school youth, both French and English, passed through Beaumont-Hamel and were told the story of Newfoundland's gallant men.

VICHTE MILITARY

I played a good many hands of cards in the front room of Joe Babstock's house, the house he built before joining the Newfoundland Regiment in 1915. Joseph, in his regimental splendour, silently watched over every hand as the cards slammed down on the chrome kitchen table. I always wondered about the neatly presented soldier in all his military glory, but my inquiries to "Grammie" about his wartime experiences were answered only with a tear. Joseph's story is intertwined with those of many of the men on the tablets and is indicative of the stories of most of the survivors. At Gueudecourt alone, where he was wounded for the first time, he lost a good friend, a neighbour, and a cousin. He was serving under Ledingham when the officer was killed at Broembeek. He bore witness to the terrible two weeks at Cambrai where he

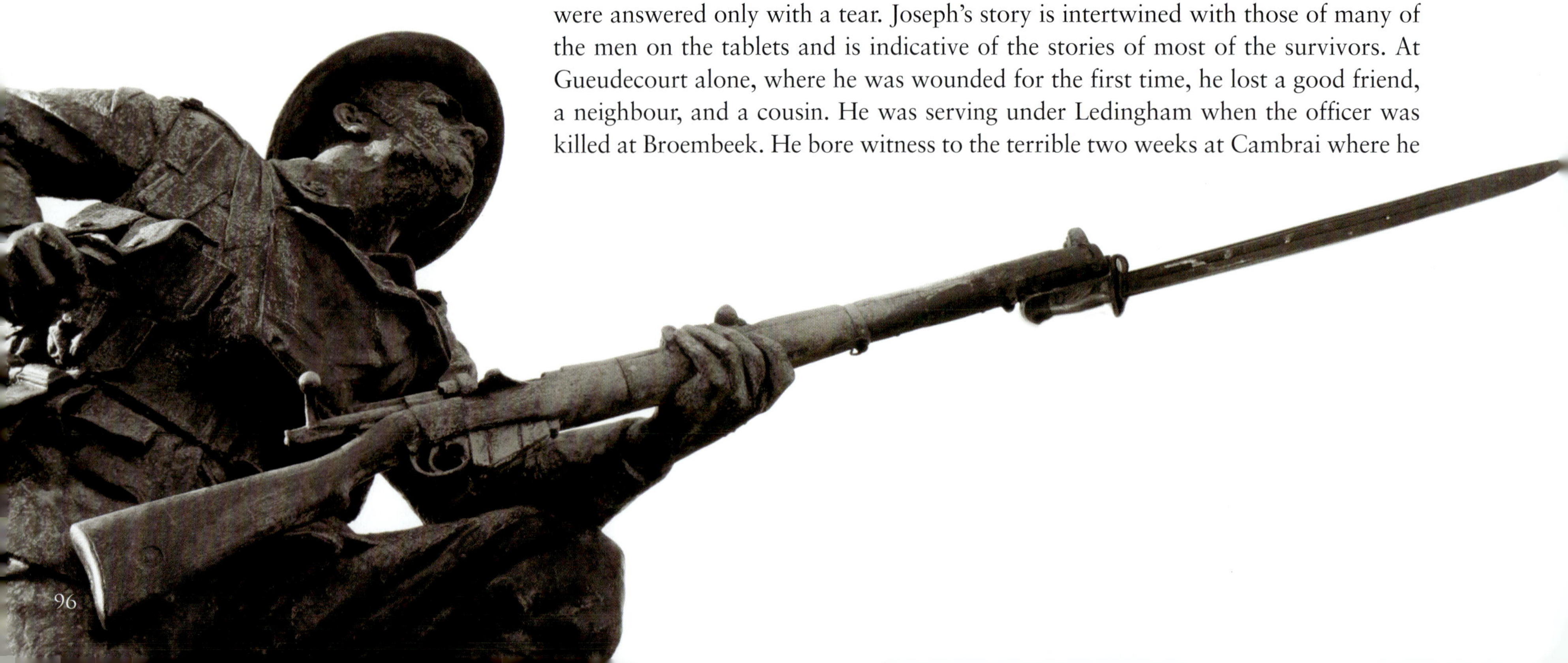

was captured and treated harshly by the Germans. He trudged and fought in the mud of Passchendaele, manned the rampart walls at Ypres, and first saw the front lines when his commanding officer was killed at Beaumont-Hamel in mid-July 1916. Joseph Babstock was one of the "lucky" veterans who returned home to a grieving nation.

It is a shame that many of the stories of these men's exploits have faded away along with those who participated. Many survivors never talked about their experiences. Certainly, the number of first-hand accounts diminishes greatly after the annihilation at Beaumont-Hamel, even though the Regiment continued to fight and earn a reputation as a crack unit. It is up to us, as Newfoundlanders and Labradorians, to keep the memory of those brave men in our collective consciousness. Hopefully, with the names of the missing returned home, more people will be interested in the story of those brave lads who, almost 100 years ago, laid down their lives in a war that was really of little concern to them, but in the end, cost them the very thing they fought for.

In the famous Notre Dame Cathedral in Paris, on a pillar near the altar, is a plaque erected by Great Britain as a memorial to the million or more men lost by the Empire, including the dominions that came to her aid, with each one represented by name and coat of arms. Listed alongside Canada, Australia, New Zealand, and South Africa is the Dominion of Newfoundland, recognized for the enormous sacrifice made by the tiny nation in the Great War.

Photo taken at Grosborn, northern Prussia, now Poland. The men are prisoners of war. Both Thistle and Babstock were captured at Cambrai, December 3, 1917, after a "terrible bombardment." It is unknown where the others were captured. Initially both Newfoundlanders were housed in the much larger Scheidemuhl (now Pila, Poland) compound but after confronting the camp commandant over working conditions and being struck with rifle butts and whips they were quickly shipped out and were told they were being sent to a punishment camp (and possibly death). Instead, 120 NCOs were housed in a small compound where conditions improved considerably. It is believed this photo commemorates the five men who confronted the Scheidemuhl Commandant.

This photo was found amongst Joseph Babstock's possessions.

(Left to Right) Walter L. Thistle, St. John's, Royal Newfoundland Regiment # 215; (possibly) Georges Geuevois, Amiens, France; Arthur Harlet of Rouen, France; Unknown (possibly Harold Manning), East Surry Regiment; Joseph Babstock, Salvage Bay (Eastport BB), Royal Newfoundland Regiment # 1847.

POURING THE BRONZE INTO MOULDS FOR THE THREE CRESTS IN NEWFOUNDLAND

Bringing them Home

by Morgan MacDonald

It is often interesting where life will take you and how events unfold in time. We are forever caught in the present, always thinking of what we are doing in our daily lives. We think of the past as if it were some distant place long ago. We can't readily see the effects of it on our daily lives. Even though we may not know it, the past does have a profound effect. The past is a book which is continually being written and we are living history today. It is only when we look back that we can see clearly that a chapter has closed and a new one is just beginning. In the present the future is always something that you hope will be better and you wonder what is to come. For the men on these tablets this was no different. They joined the war full of optimism and pride for king and country but also for a better future. Almost one hundred years ago these men had the same hopes, fears and dreams we have today. The reality of this time is hard to grasp so it must be put into perspective. Would they ever have imagined they would be forever laid to rest in the foreign fields of France and Belgium, never to return home?

We are now heading into a time in which there are no Regiment men left who can tell their stories from first-hand accounts. There is no one alive who saw these things with his own eyes or heard these sounds on the battlefield. Today it may be difficult to understand what role this history plays now and what effect it has in this time. If we take the time to learn more about their stories we can understand where we are today and where we may be in the future. Not only will these stories teach us about the world in which we live today but we can also know ourselves and who we are now.

Now, more than 90 years after these men's deaths, the names of these missing Newfoundlanders have returned home. The chapter has long since been closed on them and a new one is beginning for all of us. We can only speak from our experiences today and we can only place the Great War in terms of our own perspective and our own time. As the creators of the memorial tablets in Bowring Park our own personal journey with respect to the war started out on two parallel paths. We were first tasked with creating the tablets, but at the same time we found ourselves retracing the steps of people long past. This was our own pilgrimage to answer our own questions. Who were these men and what did they do? It is a journey that only a few fortunate people can do and a journey that everyone connected to these men should do.

Our job, Frank's and mine, was to ensure we created as close a replica as we could of the monument in France for placement in Newfoundland, so that everyone unable to travel to France to see their family names would have the chance to do so here. Overseeing our progress was the Royal Newfoundland Regiment, the Government of Newfoundland and Labrador, and also the spirit and memory of these men. Our efforts were to take careful measurements of every aspect of the tablets, photos and cross check every single name numerous times for their exactness to the monument in France, as well as to sculpt and cast portions of the tablets here.

Our emphasis was on getting it right. We were walking in the shoes of giants such as Padre Nangle, the chief driving force in the actual creation of the original monument. He was also responsible for Basil Gotto, creating the entire set of caribou we can see in France today. In effect, Nangle's legacy is that these men have a proper gravesite and memorial to honour their memory.

Monuments such as the ones placed in Bowring Park are created in a bronze casting foundry. It is hard and sometimes very hot work. To create tablets such as these, metal must be heated to the searing temperatures at which bronze becomes liquid. It is difficult because at such high temperatures most materials fail to hold their integrity. At such high temperatures, steel turns to molasses and combustibles vaporize. It is an age-old tradition and skill set that has been passed down from generation to generation and is also a skill set that cannot be taken for granted. The sculptor must be knowledgeable in the areas of metallurgy, welding, mould making, and also know the different properties of a wide array of materials.

To undertake an effort such as this, it also helps to have some well-placed experience to carry the project through the many pitfalls that can occur. Some of the bronze elements that can be seen on the tablets today were created and cast right here in Newfoundland. It is only fitting that these names could be commemorated on their home soil, and we are proud and honoured to be part of such a project.

Although these names are here from the battlefields of Europe, nothing can really replace the experience of being where these men once stood. Take the new tablets as a special commemoration and remember, but do not forget the importance of visiting the original tablets in their place of reverence far across the ocean where these men rest forever, never to come home again.

SCULPTING THE CRESTS BY HAND

UNVEILING, BOWRING PARK, NEWFOUNDLAND

Unveiling

Bowring Park, Newfoundland, July 1, 2009

The replica tablets were finally unveiled on July 1, 2009, to a standing room crowd at the Caribou monument in Bowring Park. The idea to repatriate our soldiers and sailors began in 2006 with an idea brought forth to Premier Danny Williams by then Lt. Governor Ed Roberts. Both men, along with the Regiment, made a pilgrimage to northern France and Belgium, the first time that the Royal Newfoundland Regiment paraded through the streets of France and Belgium since the end of the First World War. By all accounts it was an emotional time for everyone involved.

A lot of people, including ourselves, spent many sleepless nights leading up to the big day of the unveiling. This was not a normal contract. There were many stakeholders watching very closely, the largest, a contingent of armed infantrymen whose 592 comrades filled the main tablet. It was an honour and privilege to be among the few who made this happen. We know we have touched many of the families who waited eagerly for this day when "ours" would once again call Newfoundland home.

The late Kevin Hutchings, the Royal Newfoundland Regiment's honorary Lieutenant Colonel, said: "From now onward, people who are descendants of those who are named on these plaques can visit this site, as well as any other person who is interested in the history of our province." Clyde Jackman, Minister of Tourism, Culture, and Recreation, and Mayor of St. John's, Dennis O'Keefe, also gave stirring speeches. "There was hardly a family left unaffected by this tragic war," said Jackman. "By placing the names of these young men on the tablets here in Newfoundland and Labrador, we are, in a symbolic way, finally bringing these soldiers, sailors and other servicemen back home." The Regiment band played the "Last Post," the curtain dropped, and the boys were officially home.

After all the dignitaries had called it a day, Morgan and I stayed on a bit longer. We spoke to families who had come to witness the unveiling, bringing personal mementos and photographs. John Joseph O'Leary brought his uncle's, John Joseph Carew's, war medals; another person had placed the picture of Newfoundland Royal Naval Reservist George Stringer at the base of the tablet. We were reluctantly getting ready to leave when a low rumble broke the silence of the park. It grew louder and the first of the big bikes pulled up on the road next to the monument, followed by many more. It was a motorcycle ride led by the Canadian Army Veterans motorcycle group. They came to lay a wreath to the missing. It was a grand sight to watch as a varied group dressed in leathers, chains, and patches, and sporting greying long beards and hair, and for some, the veterans, their medals pinned to their chest as smart as any dressed member of the military, gathered around the monument. The leader gave a speech about the sacrifices of the brave men of the Royal Newfoundland Regiment, laid a wreath, and gave a salute. So long as people like them continue these acts of commemoration, we can rest assured that Newfoundland and Labrador's fallen will not be forgotten.

SPECIAL COMMEMORATION MADE BY THE CANADIAN ARMY VETERANS MOTORCYCLE GROUP AFTER THE UNVEILING

Misspelled Names

Through the research we undertook for the replication of the Beaumont-Hamel tablets and for this book, we discovered that some men's names had been misspelled. To date, there appear to be no errors on the Newfoundland Royal Naval Reserve Tablet, a testament to the fastidiousness of the British Naval record procedures. There are several mistakes on the Royal Newfoundland Regiment Tablet, and in one case the name is so badly misspelled that the man is very difficult to identify to all but his family. The Newfoundland Mercantile Marine Tablet has the most misspellings, and may actually have more, but records are scant and distributed widely.

Reasons vary for the misspellings, and we can only guess why mistakes happened. Once you access the full service records of the men on the Regiment Tablet, it becomes apparent that mistakes usually are the result of errors made by the enlistment officer who may not have been familiar with the rural speech or common names for another area of Newfoundland. Enlistment officers tended to be from England or the St. John's elite. If the names appear on this page, it is because the men have, in their own handwriting, written their names, usually on cards asking for advances to their pay or as signatures on their wills. Sometimes, it is letters from families inquiring about their son's disappearance that allow us to confirm a misspelling. It is assumed that the men knew how to spell their own names. Three men have been identified so far: Alonzo Eddy, Horatius Seward, and Joseph Teixeisa. Both Eddy and Seward came from the Clarenville area and are commemorated on the war memorial there as Alonzo Adey and Horatio Seaward, both common and correctly spelled versions. A check of both their records revealed that their names were misspelled on the memorial tablets and the memorial in Clarenville is correct. A tip from an archivist from Memorial University revealed the misspelling of Joseph Teixiesa, a Portuguese immigrant living in Pushthrough on the south coast of Newfoundland when he enlisted. His name should be spelled Teixeira, and is pronounced TAY-SHAY-DAA.

Numerous misspellings occur on the Newfoundland Mercantile Marine Tablet and were gleaned from various sources. The majority of the corrections came from customs clearing sheets that were issued prior to the vessel departing for dangerous waters overseas. Other spelling mistakes were picked up from newspapers, the *Daily News* and the *Evening Telegram*. They include Scobie Mckee, navigator for the *Cecil L. Shave*, whose name should be spelled McKie, according to the Canadian Virtual War Memorial and the *Daily News* reporting at the time of the loss of the schooner. Another, James Dooley, lost on the SS *Beverly* in 1918, had his name spelled Daly in the *Daily News* report listing the crew members of the *Beverly* alongside the Commission of Enquiry's Final Report into her sinking. The strangest set of misspelled names comes from the crew of the *Ada D. Bishop*, a schooner owned by William Ashbourne of Twillingate, from which port she cleared on her fateful journey to Gibraltar. Two of the men, Skipper Arthur Howell and sailor Mark Button, have their last names misspelled and should read Holwell and Burton, respectively. Two others have different first names for reasons that remain unclear. First Mate Rufus Burgess should read Earle M. Burgess and cook/steward Michael Atkinson should read George Atkinson.

William Pilgrim, the Master of the *Jorgina* that was lost in March 1918, may be Albert Pilgrim, Master of the *Jorgina* in the fall of 1917. It is difficult to determine as he is only commemorated on the tablets and *The Newfoundland Book of Remembrance*, and cannot be found on either the Commonwealth War Graves Commission list or the Canadian Virtual War Memorial.

There are probably more misspelled names to be found. Some may disagree with tablets being replicated verbatim, but it was the intention of everyone who pushed to have the men brought home that the tablets should not be altered in any way; their wish was to have exact replicas of the tablets in France placed on Newfoundland soil. They make no excuses, as their intention was to replicate a memorial that exists on a battlefield in France and to bring to Newfoundland and Labrador a piece of history that is as revered as the Caribou and the Danger Tree.

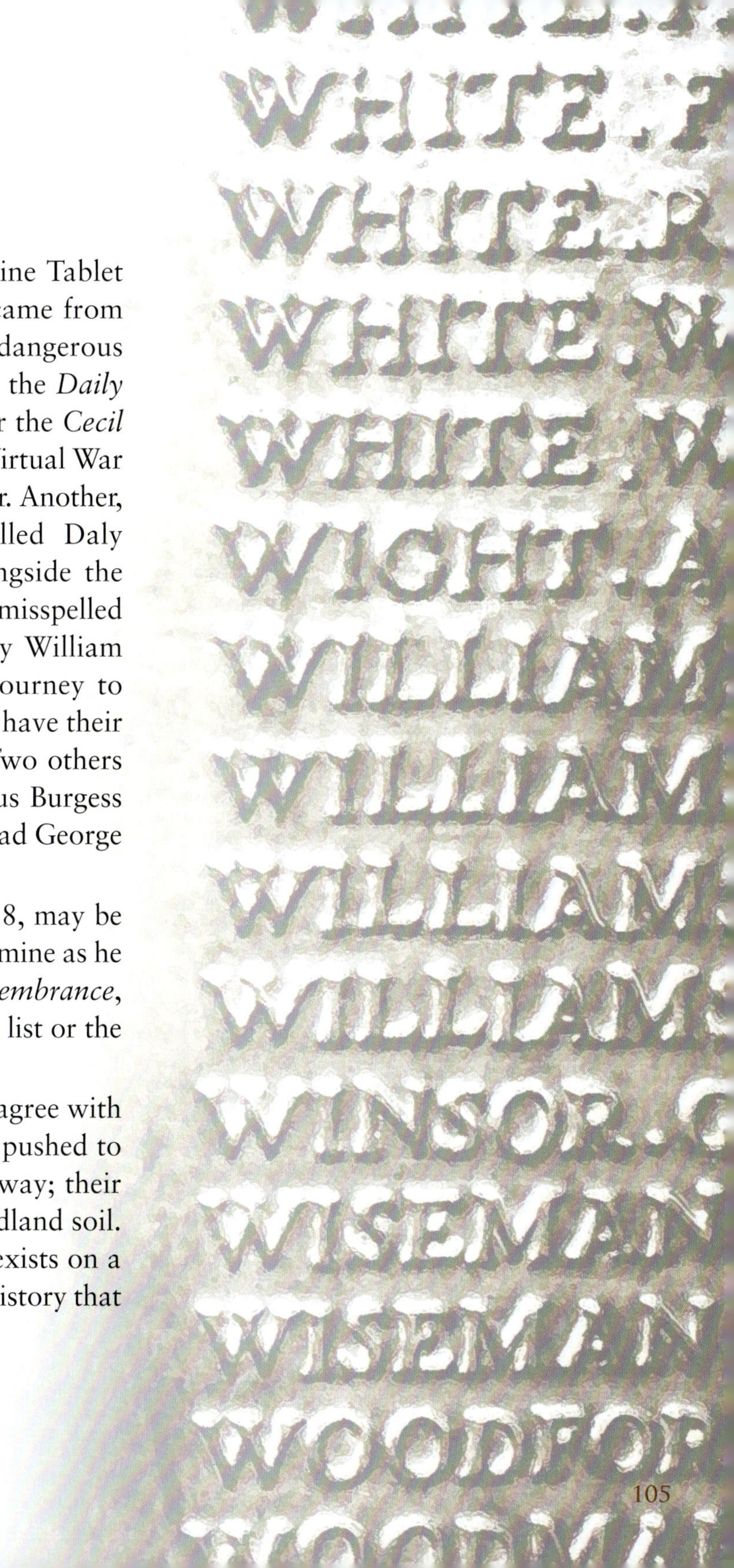

MERCANTILE MARINE — TABLET COLUMN 1

LAST NAME	FIRST NAME	PLACE OF ORIGIN	NEXT OF KIN	DATE OF DEATH	VESSEL
ALFLSEN.A.	Unknown			Jan 1 1915	SCH ANTOINETTE
ATKINSON.A	Arthur	Herring Neck	Son of Solomon	Jan 10 1918	SCH ADA D. BISHOP
ATKINSON.M.	Mark	Herring Neck	Son of Mrs. E. Atkinson	Jan 10 1918	SCH ADA D. BISHOP
BARRETT.J.	James	St. John's	Husband of Mary	Jan 21 1918	SS BEVERLY
BARRON.F.	Frank	Placentia	Son of Kate	Jan 21 1918	SS BEVERLY
BARRON.J.	James	St. John's	Husband of Julia	Jan 21 1918	SS BEVERLY
BARTLETT.I.	Isaac	Bell Island	Husband of Sarah	Oct 27 1916	SCH L.H.B
BARTLETT.M.	Mac	Bell Island	Son of Isaac, above	Oct 27 1916	SCH L.H.B
BILLARD.S.	Simeon	Rose Blanche	Husband of Emily	Dec 10 1917	SCH LIZZIE M. STANLEY
BRIELY.D.	Duncan			Jan 1 1915	BARQ LAKE SIMCOE
BREST.J.	John	Lunenburg, NS		Mar 27 1918	SS WATAGUA
BUFFETT.M.	Morgan	Burgeo	Son of Clara	Dec 10 1917	SCH LIZZIE M. STANLEY
BUFFETT.T.	Thomas	Burgeo		Dec 10 1917	SCH LIZZIE M. STANLEY
BURGESS.R.	Rufus	Burin North	Husband of Lilian	Jan 10 1918	SCH ADA D. BISHOP
BUTTON.M.	Mark	Twillingate	Son of Abel	Jan 10 1918	SCH ADA D. BISHOP
CAREW.D.	Daniel	Witless Bay	Son of Stephen	Jan 1 1915	SS LAKE SIMCOE
CARRIGAN.T.	Thomas	Logy Bay	Son of Catherine	Jan 21 1918	SS BEVERLY
CARROLL.J.	James	St. John's	Husband of Mary	Jan 15 1918	SCH ETHEL
CLARKE.S.	Solomon	Freshwater, Carbonear	Husband of Rosalia	Dec 10 1918	SCH JOHN LLEWELYN
COADY.J.	John	St. John's	Son of Margaret	Sept 1 1915	BARQ LAKE SIMCOE
COADY.W.	William			Oct 27 1916	SCH L.H.B
COOK.C.	Charles			Oct 27 1916	SCH L.H.B
COOK.H.	Harold	Port Rexton	Grandson of Honora	Nov 1 1918	SCH REVENUE
COLLIER.J.	John			Dec 10 1917	SCH LIZZIE M. STANLEY
COLLIER.W.	Ward	Burgeo		Mar 30 1918	SCH ELSIE BURDETTE
COLLINS.R.	Richard	St. John's	Son of Sarah	Jan 21 1918	SS BEVERLY
CUNNINGHAM.J.	John	St. John's		Jan 21 1918	SS BEVERLY
DEVEREAUX.A.	Andrew	Ferryland		Mar 30 1918	SS BEVERLY

LAST NAME	FIRST NAME	PLACE OF ORIGIN	NEXT OF KIN	DATE OF DEATH	VESSEL
DICKS.H.	Henry	Burgeo		Mar 30 1918	SCH ELSIE BURDETTE
DODD.J.	John	St. John's	Son of John	Jan 21 1918	SS BEVERLY
DOOLEY.J.	James	St. John's	Husband of Margaret	Jan 21 1918	SS BEVERLY
DOOLEY.M.	Michael	St. John's	Son of Patrick	Jan 10 1918	SCH W. C. MCKAY
DRISCOLL.A.	Andrew	Tors Cove		Mar 27 1918	SS WATAGUA
DUFFETT.A.	Albert	St. John's	Son of Thomas	Oct 27 1916	SCH L.H.B
EASON.W.	William	Manuels	Son of Isaac	Jan 1 1915	BARQ LAKE SIMCOE
EAVIS.A.	Alfred	Childred, Grand Bank	Son of Alfred & Amelia	Feb 1 1917	SCH DOUGLAS HAIG
EAVIS.M.	Morgan	Ramea	Nephew of Thomas F. James	Feb 1 1917	SCH DOUGLAS HAIG
EAVIS.T.	Thomas	Ramea		Feb 1 1917	SCH DOUGLAS HAIG
EVANS.H.	Hubert	St. John's		Jan 10 1918	SCH W. C. MCKAY
EVANS.J.	John	St. Jacque's		Mar 30 1918	SCH ELSIE BURDETTE
FEVER.E.	Edward			Mar 27 1918	SS WATAGUA
FLEMING.R.	Richard	Spaniard's Bay	Husband of Mary Ann	Jan 1 1915	BARQ LAKE SIMCOE
FURNEAUX.W.	William	St. John's	Son of Eliza	Jan 15 1918	SCH ETHEL
GREEN.J.	James			Feb 1 1917	SCH DOUGLAS HAIG
GREEN.R.	Robert	St. John's	Husband of Priscilla	Jan 21 1918	SS BEVERLY
HALFYARD.S.M.	Silas	St. John's	Husband of Jessie	Jan 1 1915	BARQ LAKE SIMCOE
HANCOCK.E.	Eli	39 Water St, St. John's		Mar 27 1918	SS WATAGUA
HANN.A.	Albert	Burgeo		Mar 30 1918	SCH ELSIE BURDETTE
HANN.F.	Fred	St. John's	Husband of Melinda	Jan 21 1918	SS BEVERLY
HART.C.	Charles	Fogo	Son of James	Mar 1 1918	SCH CECIL L. SHAVE
HATCHER.J.	John	Burgeo		Mar 30 1918	SCH ELSIE BURDETTE
HAWKINS.E.W.	Eli	Change Islands	Son of Mary	Dec 11 1917	SCH SIDNEY SMITH
HEARN.J.	James	St. John's	Son of Jane	Jan 21 1918	SS BEVERLY
HEARN.P.	Patrick	St. John's	Husband of Annie Croke	Jan 21 1918	SS BEVERLY
HICKMAN.C.	Chester	Grand Bank	Son of John R.	Feb 1 1917	SCH ANTOINETTE
HISCOCK.E.	Edmund	Carbonear	Husband of Margaret	Jan 1 1915	SCH JORGINA
HISCOCK.I.	Unknown	Carbonear	Son of T.	Mar 24 1918	

MERCANTILE MARINE TABLET COLUMN 2

LAST NAME	FIRST NAME	PLACE OF ORIGIN	NEXT OF KIN	DATE OF DEATH	VESSEL
HODDINOTT.W.	William	Hr Grace		Jan 1 1915	SCH ANTOINETTE
HOWELL.A.	Arthur	Herring Neck	Husband of Florence	Jan 10 1918	SCH ADA D. BISHOP
HOWELL.T.	Thomas			Mar 10 1918	SCH TATLER
HULL.H.	Hubert	Twillingate	Son of Andrew	Dec 11 1917	SCH SIDNEY SMITH
HULL.S.	Stewart	Twillingate	Son of George	Dec 11 1917	SCH SIDNEY SMITH
HUNT.R.	Robert	Greenspond	Son of Thomas	Mar 1 1918	SCH CECIL L. SHAVE
INGRAHAM.J.	Joseph	Burgeo	Husband of Annetta	Dec 10 1917	SCH LIZZIE M. STANLEY
IVEY.J.	James	St. John's	Son of Mary	Jan 15 1917	SCH ETHEL
KEAN.E.	Edgar	St. John's (Formerly Flower's Island)		Mar 1 1918	SCH CECIL L. SHAVE
KENNEY.W.	William	St. John's	Husband of Annie	Jan 21 1918	SS BEVERLY
KIRBY.P.	Patrick	St. John's	Brother of James & John	Jan 1 1915	BARQ LAKE SIMCOE
KNOTT.H.	Harold	Burgeo	Son of Mary	Dec 10 1917	SCH LIZZIE M. STANLEY
LAMBERT.F.	Frederick	Twillingate	Son of Andrew	Jan 10 1918	SCH ADA D. BISHOP
LEONARD.W.	William	British Hr TB	Husband of Annie	Mar 1 1918	SCH CECIL L. SHAVE
LEWIS.C.	Cebos	St. John's	Husband of Emma Grouchy	Jan 21 1918	SS BEVERLY
LICENCE.A.	Arthur	Stoke Ipswich England		Jan 10 1918	SCH ADA D. BISHOP
MC KEE.S.	Scobie	St. John's		Mar 1 1918	SCH CECIL L. SHAVE
MC LAUGHLIN.J.	James	Catalina	Son of Catherine	Nov 1 1918	SCH REVENUE
MC MANUS.C.	Clem	St. John's	Son of Joseph	Jan 10 1918	SCH W.C.MCKAY
MILLS.F.	Frederick	Carbonear	Son of John	Mar 24 1918	SCH JORGINA
MULLINS.H.	Harry	Catalina	Son of Bessie Manuel	Nov 1 1918	SCH REVENUE
NEIL.R.	Ralph	Spaniard's Bay	Son of Richard	Jan 1 1915	BARQ LAKE SIMCOE
NEWHOOK.E.	E	Trinity	Son of Richard	Jan 1 1915	BARQ LAKE SIMCOE
NOFTALL.J.	John	St. John's	Husband of Margaret	Jan 21 1918	SS BEVERLY
NOSEWORTHY.E.	Edward	St. John's	Son of Jessie	Jan 15 1918	SCH ETHEL
O'BRIEN.J.	James	Carbonear	Brother of Margaret Mabel	Mar 24 1918	SCH JORGINA
O'NEILL.W.	William	St. John's		Jan 10 1918	SCH W.C.MCKAY
OSMOND.C.	Ceaf	Carbonear	Son of George	Mar 24 1918	SCH JORGINA

LAST NAME	FIRST NAME	PLACE OF ORIGIN	NEXT OF KIN	DATE OF DEATH	VESSEL
OWEN.R.	Richard	St. John's		Mar 27 1918	SS WATAGUA
PEDDLE.E.	Eli	Haystack	Son of John	Jan 21 1918	SS BEVERLY
PENDER.C.	Cornelius	St. John's	Son of Ann	Jan 21 1918	SS BEVERLY
PENNEY.S.	Sim	Catalina	Son of Catherine	Nov 1 1918	SCH REVENUE
PEPPAS.H.N.	H N			Jan 1 1915	BARQ LAKE SIMCOE
PILGRIM.W.	William			Mar 24 1918	SCH JORGINA
PORTER.H.	Henry	Change Islands	Son of Maria	Dec 11 1917	SCH RUMFORD
POWER.J.	John	Outer Cove	Son of John Camp	Jan 21 1918	SS BEVERLY
ROWE.F.	Frederick	Bell Island	Husband of Louise King	Feb 1 1918	SCH MORAN
RYAN.A.	Albert	Salmonier	Son of John	Jan 21 1918	SS BEVERLY
SHEEHAN.J.	John			Oct 27 1916	SCH L.H.B
SHORT.S.	Samuel	Small Point, CBN	Son of William	Mar 24 1918	SCH JORGINA
SHUTE.S.	Stephen	Freshwater, CBN		Jan 1 1915	SCH ANTOINETTE
SMITH.N.	Noah	Manuels	Husband of Martha	Jan 1 1915	BARQ LAKE SIMCOE
SPRACKLIN.T.	Thomas	St. John's	Nephew of Charlotte	Jan 15 1918	SCH ETHEL
STEWART.J.	John	North Strand Drogheda Ireland		Jan 10 1918	SCH W.C.MCKAY
STEWART.P.	Peter	St. John's	Husband of Helen	Jan 21 1918	SS BEVERLY
STRICKLAND.W.	Ward	Burgeo		Mar 30 1918	SCH ELSIE BURDETTE
SUTTON.J.	John	St. John's		Nov 1 1918	SCH REVENUE
TAYLOR.G.	Gus	Carbonear	Son of Duncan	Dec 11 1917	SCH SIDNEY SMITH
TORRES.JOSE.	Jose De La Cruz	Chancho, Chile	Son of Maria Avela	Jan 10 1918	SCH W.C.MCKAY
TURPIN.J.	John	St. John's		Mar 1 1918	SCH CECIL L. SHAVE
WALSH.M.	Michael	Catalina	Son of Bridget	Nov 1 1918	SCH REVENUE
WALSH.P.	Patrick	St. John's	Husband of Veronica	Jan 21 1918	SS BEVERLY
WEBBER.G.	George	Hr Grace		Jan 1 1915	SCH ANTOINETTE
WELLS.H.	Hubert	Twillingate	Phillip & Lucy	Dec 11 1917	SCH SIDNEY SMITH
WHITE.J.	John	St. John's	Husband of Harriet	Jan 15 1918	SCH ETHEL
WHITE.T.	Thomas	St. John's	Husband of Annie	Jan 1 1915	BARQ LAKE SIMCOE
WILSON.A.SNR	Capt Andrew	St. John's	Husband of Mary	Jan 21 1918	SS BEVERLY
WILSON.A.JNR	Andrew	St. John's	Son of Mary	Jan 21 1918	SS BEVERLY

Royal Newfoundland Regiment Tablet Column 1

Last Name and Rank	First Name	Reg #	Place of Origin	Next of Kin	Battle	Age	Date of Death
2nd Lieutenant							
ALCOCK.A.	Augustus	1372	Griguet	Mark & Mary	Monchy-le-Preux	21	Apr 14 1917
AYRE.G.W.	Gerald Walter		St. John's	Fred. Wm & Mary Julia	Beaumont-Hamel	25	Jul 1 1916
Private							
ABBOTT.E.	Eli	2119	Grand Falls	Charles & Ann	Sailly-Saillisel	19	Jan 28 1917
ABBOTT.F.	Frederick	3483	Musgrave Hr	Walter & Jane	Steenbeek	20	Aug 16 1917
ABBOTT.G.	George	1242	Battery Rd, St. John's	Henry & Emily	Beaumont-Hamel	22	Jul 1 1916
ABBOTT.S.	Stanley	283	Battery Rd, St. John's	Henry & Emily	Beaumont-Hamel	21	Jul 1 1916
ADAMS.O.H.	Otto Herbert	1770	31 Lemarchant Rd, St. John's	Ths. Dan. & Theresa Fr.	Broembeek	18	Oct 9 1917
ADAMS.W.	William	2306	Arnold's Cove	James & Alister Ann	Monchy-le-Preux	17	Apr 14 1917
ANDREWS.J.	Joseph	1119	St. John's	Son of Catherine	Beaumont-Hamel		Jul 1 1916
ANDREWS.W.	Walter	2058	St. John's	John S & Emma	Masnieres	19	Nov 20 1917
ANTLE.G.	Gilbert	1899	Botwood	Thomas & Mary	Beaumont-Hamel	21	Jul 1 1916
ARNOLD.C.G.	Chesley Gladstone	1386	Traytown, Alexander Bay	Wm & Alice	Monchy-le-Preux	24	Apr 14 1917
Captain M.C. & BAR.CAVALIER CROWN OF ITALY							
BARTLETT.R.W.	Rupert		Brigus	Wm J & Mary	Marcoing	26	Nov 30 1917
2ndLieut.BARRETT.H.G..M.M.	Harold George	798	St. John's	Son of H.G.	Steenbeek		Aug 16 1917
Coy.Q.M.Sergeant							
BASTOW.G.C.	Gordon Clarence	930	St. John's	Marldon & Fanny	Gueudecourt	22	Oct 11 1916
Sergeant							
BENDELL.J.A.	James Alexander	207	St. John's	Wm & Sophia	Broembeek	22	Oct 9 1917
BESON.P.	Patrick	2232	Joe Batt's Arm	Son of James	Monchy-le-Preux	29	Apr 14 1917
BOOTH.J.	John	2405	Peterhead, Scotland	James & Jessie	Monchy-le-Preux	27	Apr 14 1917
BROWN.B.	Bertram	1382	Grand Falls	Amos & Selina	Beaumont-Hamel	21	Jul 1 1916
BURRY.S.G.	Sidney George	1044	Greenspond	Job & Matilda	Beaumont-Hamel	31	Jul 1 1916
BURT.C.	Charles	2647	Rose Blanche	Andrew & Kate	Bailleul	26	Apr 13 1918
Corporal							
BEST.F.G..M.M.	Frank Gordon	42	Tack's Beach, Placentia Bay	Son of Josiah	Broembeek		Oct 9 1917

LAST NAME AND RANK	FIRST NAME	REG #	PLACE OF ORIGIN	NEXT OF KIN	BATTLE	AGE	DATE OF DEATH
LANCE CORPORAL							
BENNETT.H.	Hector	910	Stephenville	Luke A. & Josephine	Monchy-le-Preux	20	Apr 14 1917
BENNETT.W..D.C.M.	William	1071	Stephenville	Luke A. & Josephine	Monchy-le-Preux	22	Apr 14 1917
BRYANT.A.	Aaron	847	Whiteway, TB	Son of Mary Elizabeth	Sailly-Saillisel	26	Jan 28 1917
BULGIN.A..M.M.	Augustus	2427	Farmer's Arm, Twillingate	John & Susan	Bailleul	23	Apr 13 1918
BURSEY.G.	George	2677	Victoria Cove, Gander Bay	Andrew& Isabella	Keiberg	23	Oct 2 1918
PRIVATE							
BADCOCK.A.	Arthur	2314	Bay Roberts	Rich. & Susie	Sailly-Saillisel	19	Mar 3 1917
BAKER.E.	Esau	3696	Clarenville	Caleb & Theresa	Marcoing	30	Dec 3 1917
BAKER.G.	George	1439	Clarenville	Caleb & Theresa	Broembeek	21	Oct 9 1917
BALDWIN.U.	Uriah	1846	Pouch Cove	Edward & Alice	Broembeek	23	Oct 9 1917
BALLAM.A.G.	Arthur	3031	Curling	Manoah & Alice	Marcoing	19	Dec 3 1917
BAMBURY.S.	Samuel	3571	Poole's Cove	George & Elvina	Bailleul	20	Apr 12 1918
BARNES.L.	Lawrence	528	St. John's	Wm & Mary	Steenbeek		Aug 14 1917
BARNES.M.	Maxwell	1576	Topsail	Son of Ms. Sarah Ann	Beaumont-Hamel	22	Jul 1 1916
BARRETT.L J	Leonard Joseph	372	St. John's	Son of Maud	Beaumont-Hamel		Jul 1 1916
BARTLETT.J.P.	Joseph Patrick	629	Maryvale Brigus	Son of John	Beaumont-Hamel		Jul 1 1916
BARTON.J.	John	1485	The Goulds (Bay Bull's Road)	Wm & Annie	Beaumont-Hamel	29	Jul 1 1916
BENNETT.C.	Chesley	3519	Lewisporte	James& Alice	Masnieres	17	Nov 20 1917
BENNETT.P.F.	Peter Francis	770	St. John's	Joseph & Margaret	Monchy-le-Preux	25	Apr 14 1917
BENNETT.W.	William	1229	St. John's	Wm & Agnes	Beaumont-Hamel	31	Jul 1 1916
BENOIT.B.	Benjamin	3531	Conne River	John & Margaret	Masnieres	21	Nov 20 1917
BENOIT.W.	Walter	2683	Stephenville Crossing	John & Olive	Monchy-le-Preux	22	Apr 14 1917
BENSON.W.	Wilson	3357	South Side, St John's	Newman & Sarah	Marcoing	17	Dec 3 1917
BISHOP.A.W.	Archibald	1046	Burin North	Frederick James & Mary Bridget	Masnieres	21	Nov 20 1917
BISHOP.C.G.	Caleb Golding	2524	Mundy Pond Rd, St. John's	Jacob & Eliza Mary	Monchy-le-Preux	19	Apr 14 1917
BLACKMORE.E.	Edgar	1578	Pilley's Island	Henry & Fanny	Monchy-le-Preux	21	Apr 14 1917
BLANDFORD.G.	George	3237	Port Albert	Eli & Selina/wife WG King	Steenbeek	23	Aug 14 1917

Royal Newfoundland Regiment Tablet Column 2

LAST NAME AND RANK	FIRST NAME	REG #	PLACE OF ORIGIN	NEXT OF KIN	BATTLE	AGE	DATE OF DEATH
BOBBETT.M.	Matthew	3541	McCallum	Son of John	Ypres 1918	18	Mar 13 1918
BOLLARD.G.E.	George	2334	Bollard's Town, Sound Island,PB	John & Susan	Monchy-le-Preux	26	Apr 14 1917
BOONE.J.	Joseph	3478	Leading Tickles, West Twillingate	John & Luisa	Bailleul	20	Apr 18 1917
BOUTCHER.J.	John	5940	Mussel Hr Arm, PB	Reuben & Emma	Died at Sea	24	Oct 9 1918
BOWMAN.C.	Charles	938	St. John's	Son of Frigaz	Beaumont-Hamel	26	Jul 1 1916
BOYD.A.	Alphonso	2745	Tizzard's Hr	Son of Edward	Monchy-le-Preux	19	Apr 14 1917
BREEN.J.	John	67	St. John's	Jacob & Catherine Kane	Beaumont-Hamel	20	Jul 1 1916
BRENT.D.	David	1794	Botwood	Son of John	Beaumont-Hamel	23	Jul 1 1916
BRINSTON.A.P.	Augustus Perry	2851	Bay Bull's Arm, TB	Nelson & Hannah	Steenbeek	19	Aug 16 1917
BRINSTON.G.	George	1772	North Harbour, PB	Rb Wm & Amelia Jane	Broembeek	17	Oct 9 1917
BROCKLEHURST.G.A.	George Augustus	848	St. John's	Charles F & Mary Ann	Steenbeek	30	Aug 16 1917
BROWN.E.J.	Edward John	545	Harbour Grace	Eli & Annie	Beaumont-Hamel	28	Jul 1 1916
BROWN.L.	Louis	2044	Bishop's Harbour, BB	Henry & Hannah	Gueudecourt	18	Oct 11 1916
BROWN.O.	Orlando	2670	Trinity East	Wm & Sarah	Sailly-Saillisel	19	Feb 25 1917
BROWN.W.	William	2183	Little Hr, Twilligate	Brother of Eliza Keefe/ Son of Annie Reff	Gueudecourt	25	Oct 12 1916
BRYANT.C.	Charles	3623	Hickman's Hr	Herbert & Drucilla	Bailleul	18	Apr 12 1918
BUCKLEY.J.	James	4274	Botwood	Son of John	Ingoyghem		Oct 25 1918
BUGDEN.F.	Frederick	3873	Epworth, Burin	Fletcher & Olivia	Bailleul	17	Apr 13 1918
BUGDEN.J.S.	John Stanley	2815	Epworth, Burin	Henry & Elizabeth	Masnieres	20	Nov 20 1917
BUGDEN.L.	Leighton	1544	St. John's	James & Bessie	Gueudecourt	21	Oct 12 1916
BURGE.A.	Allen	624	Bonavista	George & Mary Jane	Beaumont-Hamel	20	Jul 1 1916
BURT.E.	Eric	1152	St. John's	John & Jemima	Broembeek	20	Oct 9 1917
BURTON.A.	Andrew	3776	Beaumont North, Twillingate	George & Julia	Bailleul	20	Apr 13 1918
BURTON.G.L.	George Lewis	2415	Hr Buffett	George & Eliza	Monchy-le-Preux	27	Apr 14 1917
BUTT.D.	Dorman	3692	Exploits	Son of Thomas	Marcoing	26	Dec 3 17
BUTT.E.	Edward	1623	Child's Point, Bay of Islands	James & Sophia	Monchy-le-Preux	19	Apr 14 1917
BUTLER.I.J.	Ignatus Joseph	1442	St. George	Son of Mary C	Beaumont-Hamel		Jul 1 1916
BUTLER.J.J.	James	1289	Shoal Hr	Zachariah & Elizabeth	Monchy-le-Preux		Apr 14 1917
BUTLER.R.	Robert	1282	Bay Roberts	John Thomas & Emily	Gueudecourt	23	Oct 11 1916
BUTLER.T.C.	Thomas Charles	2990	Griquet	Garland & Sarah	Sailly-Saillisel	29	Mar 2 1917
BUTLER.W.	Wilson	2938	Flat Islands, PB	Samuel & Jane	Broembeek	24	Oct 9 1917

LAST NAME AND RANK	FIRST NAME	REG #	PLACE OF ORIGIN	NEXT OF KIN	BATTLE	AGE	DATE OF DEATH
Lieutenant							
CLIFT.C.B.	Cecil Bayly	505	St. John's	James Augustus & Agne	Gueudecourt	24	Oct 12 1916
Sergeant							
COUGHLAN.L.	Louis	2256	St. John's	Son of James	Monchy-le-Preux	22	Apr 14 1917
Corporal							
CARROLL.B..M.M.	Bernard	1903	Conche, French Shore	Dan & Elizabeth	Monchy-le-Preux	24	Apr 14
CAVE.J.	Joseph	2944	Change Islands	Elias & Lucy	Ypres 1917	24	Jul 10 1917
CHRISTOPHER.L.J	Leo Joseph	1783	St. Joseph's, Salmonier	Michael & Catherine	Broembeek	17	Oct 9 1917
CLARE.L.E.	Lawrence Edward	343	St. John's	John & Margaret	Gueudecourt	22	Oct 12 1916
COOK.A.S.	Alfred Stanley	876	Southside, St Johns	Wm James & Emily	Monchy-le-Preux	26	Apr 14 1917
Lance Corporal							
COLBOURNE.B.S.	Beaton	1675	Bishop's Falls	Edwin B & Ellen	Monchy-le-Preux	32	Apr 14 1917
CRANE.N.	Nathaniel	363	Upper Island Cove	Nathaniel & Mary Esther	Monchy-le-Preux	21	Apr 14 1917
Private							
CAHILL.M.J.	Martin Joseph	258	Bell Island	John & Mary Sweeney	Beaumont-Hamel	25	Jul 1 1916
CALLAHAN.R.J.	Rodger John	344	St. John's	Son of Rodger	Beaumont-Hamel		Jul 1 1916
CANNING.C.	Charles	3466	Caplin Bay, Ferryland	Alfred & Mary	Bailleul	26	Apr 13 1918
CAREW.J.J.	John Joseph	1028	2 Brien Street, St. John's	John Michael & Elizabeth	Beaumont-Hamel	24	Jul 1 1916
CAREW.V.	Victor	1560	Shores Cove, Cape Broyle	Henry J & Esther	Masnieres	24	Nov 20 1917
CHAFE.G.	George	3236	St. John's	Philip & Jane W/wife Jane	Bailleul	35	Apr 13 1918
CHAFFEY.A.J.	Arthur James	3014	Jeffrey's, Bay St George	Edward & Catherine Ann	Marcoing	19	Dec 3 1917
CHATMAN.A.	Albert	2278	Bunyan's Cove, BB	William & Olive	Masnieres	26	Nov 20 1917
CHAYTOR.C.	Charles	3168	Greenspond	Son of Elizabeth Hoddinot	Marcoing	22	Dec 3 1917
CHUCK.G.	George	2497	Russia	John & Mary	Monchy-le-Preux	23	Apr 14 1917
CLARK.W.	William	2268	Kerley's Hr	Joseph & Mary Elizabeth	Monchy-le-Preux	20	Apr 14 1917

Royal Newfoundland Regiment

Tablet Column 3

LAST NAME AND RANK	FIRST NAME	REG #	PLACE OF ORIGIN	NEXT OF KIN	BATTLE	AGE	DATE OF DEATH
CLARKE.G.S.	George	2541	Springdale	George W & Rosanna	Broembeek	20	Oct 9 1917
CLARKE.T.	Thomas	3311	The Goulds	John & Bridget	Ypres 1917	18	Sep 28 1917
CLARKE.W.J.	Walter	2574	Springdale	George W & Rosanna	Monchy-le-Preux	23	Apr 14 1917
CLEARY.B.	Bernard	1359	Harbour Main	Edward & Ellen (Ezekial remarried)	Beaumont-Hamel	19	Jul 1 1916
CLEARY.P.M.	Patrick Michael	1230	St. John's	John & Jane	Gueudecourt	23	Oct 12 1916
COISH.H.G.	Harold Gordon	1400	Ladle Cove, Fogo	Wm & Maud	Beaumont-Hamel	21	Jul 1 1916
COLE.E.L.	Edward Louis	195	Elliston	Ed. Jas & Fanny Jane	Trench Raid	18	Jun 28 1916
COLES.A.V.	Albert	1813	Flower's Cove	Matthew & Sarah	Ypres 1916	22	Sep 18 1916
COLLINS.G.W.	George	2448	St. John's	James Joseph & Bridget	Monchy-le-Preux	19	Apr 14 1917
COLLINS.J.	James	567	Jerseyside PB	John R & Elizabeth	Monchy-le-Preux	20	Apr 14 1917
COLLINS.L.J.	Leo James	2952	St. John's	Son of James	Steenbeek	19	Aug 16 1917
COLLINS.M.B.	Martin Bertram	913	Placentia	Michael & Annie J.	Broembeek	21	Oct 9 1917
COLUMBUS.F.	Frank	2296	St. Georges	Francis & Susan	Broembeek	21	Oct 9 1917
CONNORS.D.F.	Daniel Francis	649	Pouch Cove	David & Jane	Monchy-le-Preux	23	Apr 14 1917
CONNORS.J.P.	James Patrick	209	St. John's	Patrick & Mary Ann	Beaumont-Hamel	23	Jul 1 1916
CONNORS.M.G.	Maurice Gregory	3942	Conception Harbour	Patrick & Ann	Bailleul	22	Apr 13 1918
COOK.H.W.	Henry William	483	St. John's	Henry Rex & Jessie	Gueudecourt	20	Oct 12 1916
COOPER.P.	Peter	786	St. John's	Peter J & Margaret	Broembeek	27	Oct 9 1917
COOPER.W.M.	Ward Mellage	1945	Millertown	John & Annie Jone(for Cooper)	Broembeek	20	Oct 9 1917
COX.W.	William	2989	Hr Breton, Fortune	William & Amelia	Masnieres	24	Nov 20 1917
CORCORAN.L.J.	Laurence Joseph	1635	St. John's	La. Jos. & Julia	Beaumont-Hamel	33	Jul 1 1916
COULTAS.N.	Norman	1058	St. John's	Myles & Maria	Beaumont-Hamel	17	Jul 1 1916
CRANE.J.	Joseph	2313	Tilton, CB	Wm Henry& Wilhelmina	Monchy-le-Preux	24	Apr 14 1917
CRANFORD.J.F.	James	2221	St. John's	Son of Wm	Monchy-le-Preux	27	Apr 14 1917
CRANFORD.L.G.	Llewelyn	163	New Hr, TB	John & Flora	Beaumont-Hamel	24	Jul 1 1916
CROCKER.H	Harrison	1186	Heart's Delight	Sam & Emily	Beaumont-Hamel	25	Jul 1 1916
CROCKER.J	Job	2418	Heart's Delight	John & Honora	Monchy-le-Preux	19	Apr 14 1917
CRON.J.M.	James Matthew	1585	Hr Grace	James & Emma	Monchy-le-Preux	18	Apr 14 1917
CROUCHER.N.	Nathaniel	1495	Cutwell, NDB	Elias & Hagar	Beaumont-Hamel	19	Jul 1 1916
CUFF.G.L.	George Lettle	630	Bonavista	Wm & Deborah	Monchy-le-Preux	24	Apr 14 1917
CURLEY.J.T.	John Thomas	1435	Wood's Is, Bay of Islands	Phillip & Ann	Beaumont-Hamel	35	Jul 1 1916
CURTIS.A.	Archibald	2449	Port Blandford	James & Susannah	Monchy-le-Preux	25	Apr 14 1917

LAST NAME AND RANK	FIRST NAME	REG #	PLACE OF ORIGIN	NEXT OF KIN	BATTLE	AGE	DATE OF DEATH
CORPORAL							
DOYLE.J.T..	John Thomas	1014	King's Cove	Edward & Lucy	Beaumont-Hamel	25	Jul 1 1916
LANCE CORPORAL							
DUNPHY.J.J.	John Joseph	2459	St. John's	Patrick & Ellen	Somme 1916	21	Nov 29 1916
DUNPHY.T.P.	Thomas	2155	St. John's	John & Maria	Sailly-Saillisel	20	Mar 2 1917
PRIVATE							
DAWE.F.	Fred	3334	Kelligrews	Ambrose & Jane	Ypres 1917	25	Sep 28 1917
DAY.J.L.	James Lewis	1484	St. John's	Ernest & Sarah	Les Fosses Farm/Monchy	19	Apr 23 1917
DELANEY.T.J.	Thomas	2225	Placentia	Michael & Bridget	Masnieres	19	Nov 20 1917
DE LOUCHREY.H.	Harold	196	Little Bay, NDB	Jo. & Frances	Somme 1916	19	Nov 29 1916
DENTY.H.	Herbert	2598	Traytown	Simon & Elizabeth	Monchy-le-Preux	22	Apr 14 1917
DEVEREAUX.A.	Aiden	3135	Ferryland	James & Mary	Masnieres	20	Nov 20 1917
DICKS.A.	Almer	3539	Hr Buffett	Fred & Clara	Ingoyghem	21	Oct 25 1918
DICKS.B.	Benjamin	2828	Burgeo	Wm & Susie	Monchy-le-Preux	18	Apr 14 1917
DOMINY.H.	Harry	3769	Greenspond	Edgar & Annie	Ypres 1918	19	Mar 14 1918
DONNELLY.W.	Willliam	2162	St. John's	Wm & Mary	Monchy-le-Preux	19	Apr 14 1917
DORAN.J.	Joseph	1551	Trepassey	Edward & Mary	Monchy-le-Preux	30	Apr 14 1917
DOWDEN.H.	Henry	2326	Rock Hr, Burin	Eli & Ann	Monchy-le-Preux	21	Apr 14 1917
DRISCOLL.A.	Arthur	1054	St. John's	Absalom & Virtue	Beaumont-Hamel	20	Jul 1 1916
DULLANTY.G.	George	1096	St. John's	Son of Thomas	Les Beoufs/Somme		Nov 21 1916
DUNPHY.E.L.	Edmond	2967	St. John's	Patrick & Ellen	Monchy-le-Preux	17	Apr 14 1917
SERGEANT							
ELLIOTT.W.S.	William Skeffington	1073	Newman's Cove, BB	Albert & Annie	Beaumont-Hamel	22	Jul 1 1916

ROYAL NEWFOUNDLAND REGIMENT TABLET COLUMN 4

LAST NAME AND RANK	FIRST NAME	REG #	PLACE OF ORIGIN	NEXT OF KIN	BATTLE	AGE	DATE OF DEATH
LANCE CORPORAL							
ELLIS.J.J.	John Joseph	443	St. John's	JJ & Annie	Beaumont-Hamel	22	Jul 1 1916
EZEKIEL.J.	Joseph	1336	Harbour Main	Paul & Lucy	Gueudecourt	25	Oct 12 1916
PRIVATE							
EBBS.J.	John	2351	St. John's	John & Agnes	Les Beoufs/Somme	19	Nov 21 1916
EDDY.A.	Alonzo	2384	Clarenville	John & Bertha	Monchy-le-Preux	19	Apr 14 1917
EDGAR.E.	Edwin	737	Greenspond	Edwin & Helen	Beaumont-Hamel	35	Jul 1 1916
EDGECOMBE.E.F.	Edward Francis	40	Catalina	Rueben & Elizabeth	Ypres 1917	19	Aug 21 1917
EDNEY.S.R.	Samuel	1714	St. John's	Son of John T	Gueudecourt	29	Oct 12 1916
ELLIS.A.	Ambrose	3809	Port Saunders	Thomas & Fanny	Bailleul	29	Apr 13 1918
ELLIOTT.G.	George	2737	WinterBrook, BB	Alex & Elizabeth	Marcoing	20	Dec 3 1917
ELLIOTT.J.	John	22	St. John's	John & Elizabeth	Beaumont-Hamel	18	Jul 1 1916
ELLSWORTH.J.T.	John	2469	Carmanville	Moses & Lenora	Monchy-le-Preux	23	Apr 14 1917
EMBERLY.G.	George	2994	English Hr East	Patrick & Margaret	Broembeek	23	Oct 8 1917
ENGLAND.H.S.	Hugh	3858	St George	Wm George & Annie	Ypres 1918	24	Mar 13 1918
ETHERIDGE.G.	Gordon	1858	Champney's East, TB	John & Priscilla	Beaumont-Hamel	24	Jul 1 1916
ETHERIDGE.R.	Richard	1345	Joe Batt's Arm	Richard & Theresa	Ypres, 1918		Mar 28 1918
EVANS.H.	Henry	1245	Adams Cove		Beaumont-Hamel		Jul 1 1916
EVANS.L.	Leonard	658	Bay Roberts	Jabez & Elizabeth	Gueudecourt	25	Oct 12 1916
EVANS.N.	Nicholas	1767	St. John's	Luke & Mary	Beaumont-Hamel	20	Jul 1 1916
EVOY.F.	Francis	2202	Harricott, St Mary's Bay	Thomas & Martha	Sailly-Saillisel	29	Jan 28 1917
2ND LIEUTENANT							
FERGUSON.J.R.	John Roy	882	Millertown	Daniel & Isabella/ Wife Jeannette	Beaumont-Hamel	27	Jul 1 1916
SERGEANT							
FERGUSON.S.S.	Stewart Small	95	St. John's	Daniel & Isabella	Beaumont-Hamel	26	Jul 1 1916
CORPORAL							
FREW.M.	Mackintosh	2246	Grand Falls	Wm & Katie	Monchy-le-Preux	19	Apr 14 1917

LAST NAME AND RANK	FIRST NAME	REG #	PLACE OF ORIGIN	NEXT OF KIN	BATTLE	AGE	DATE OF DEATH
PRIVATE							
FALLON.S.	Stephen	1191	Harbour Grace	John & Susie	Beaumont-Hamel	17	Jul 1 1916
FARRELL.M.P.	Martin Patrick	1798	Marystown	John & Mary	Beaumont-Hamel	19	Jul 1 1916
FIELD.J	John	2003	St. John's		Gueudecourt	20	Oct 12 1916
FIELDS.C.	Charles	3267	Cook's Hr, Str Belle Isle	Foster son of Fanny Bradbury	Broembeek	33	Oct 9 1917
FILLIER.F.	Frank	1377	Petty Hr	Son of Thomas	Beaumont-Hamel		Jul 1 1916
FITZGERALD.T.J.	Thomas Joseph	1645	Ropewalk Range, St. John's	Thomas Joseph & Elizabeth	Monchy-le-Preux	19	Apr 14 1917
FLEMING.R.	Richard	1594	Bell Island		Les Fosses Farm/Monchy	23	Apr 23 1917
FOLLETT.A.	Albert	2920	Grand Beach, Burin	Wm & Parthena	Monchy-le-Preux	20	Apr 14 1917
FORD.G.	Gerald	1559	Amherst Cove	George & Sarah	Beaumont-Hamel	22	Jul 1 1916
FORTUNE.W.	William	1194	Tors Cove	Son of Sylvester	Monchy-le-Preux	26	Apr 14 1917
FORWARD.N.	Norman	2067	Tizzard's Hr	Obediah & Priscilla	Sailly-Saillisel	21	Mar 2 1917
FRAMPTON.H.	Harry	2198	Grand Falls	George & Sarah	Monchy-le-Preux	23	Apr 14 1917
FRANCIS.A.E.	Albert Edward	2918	Hermitage Cove	Philip & Susan	Monchy-le-Preux	22	Apr 14 1917
FRENCH.J.J.	John Joseph	63	Brigus North	Ben. & Bridget	Beaumont-Hamel	25	Jul 1 1916
FRY.J.	John	2734	St. John's	Son of Enoch	Masnieres	25	Nov 20 1917
FUDGE.J.	Jeremiah	2839	Pass Is, Fortune Bay	James & Rosanna	Monchy-le-Preux	22	Apr 14 1917
LIEUTENANT							
GOODYEAR.S.C..M.C.	Stanley Charles	369	Grand Falls	Josiah & Louisa	Broembeek	31	Oct 10 1917
2ND LIEUTENANT							
GARDNER.C..D.C.M. & BAR	Cyril		British Harbour	Arthur & Mary	Monchy-le-Preux	32	Apr 14 1917
SERGEANT							
GEAR.J.J.	James Joseph	695	St. John's	Son of Agnes Fitzpatrick	Monchy-le-Preux	21	Apr 14 1917
GULLAGE.H.V.	Hubert Victor	1682	Catalina	Peter	Gueudecourt	20	Oct 12 1916
CORPORAL							
GRANT.E.P.	Edward Peter	1797	Lawn	Michael & Mary	Steenbeek	24	Aug 16 1917
GUY.C.C.	Chester Cameron	1475	Burgeo	Son of John Robert	Beaumont-Hamel		Jul 1 1916
LANCE CORPORAL							
GALLOP.M.	Morgan	2434	St. John's	Son of Mrs Kennedy	Bailleul	20	Apr 13 1918
GARDNER.E.J.	Edward James	1247	British Harbour	Arthur & Mary	Beaumont-Hamel	25	Jul 1 1916

Royal Newfoundland Regiment Tablet Column 5

LAST NAME AND RANK	FIRST NAME	REG #	PLACE OF ORIGIN	NEXT OF KIN	BATTLE	AGE	DATE OF DEATH
GILLAM.A.W.	Arthur Wilfred	454	Robinson's Head	Son of Charles	Beaumont-Hamel		Jul 1 1916
GOSSE.T.J.	Thomas Joseph	1051	Torbay	Samuel & Ellen	Monchy-le-Preux	21	Apr 14 1917
GOUGH.C.J.	Chesley James	893	Elliston	Son of James	Gueudecourt	23	Oct 12 1916
PRIVATE							
GALGAY.F.J.	Francis Joseph	892	St. John's	Francis & Mary	Beaumont-Hamel	19	Jul 1 1916
GEORGE.J.	Joshua	2015	Foster's Point, Random TB	Noah & Elizabeth	Gueudecourt	22	Oct 12 1916
GILBERT.A.	Alexander	2891	Come By Chance	Albert & Katherine	Sailly-Saillisel	21	Mar 2 1917
GILLESPIE.S.J.	Samuel Joseph	3195	Fortune Hr, NDB	Son of John	Bailleul	22	Apr 13 1918
GILLINGHAM.C.	Charles	1445	Ochre Pit Cove	John Sam. & Naomi	Ypres 1917	24	Sep 28 1917
GOSS.S.	Samuel	1907	Torbay	Peter & Mary	Monchy-le-Preux	24	Apr 14 1917
GOSSE.I.J.	Ira Joseph	716	St. John's	Joseph & Margaret	Gueudecourt	23	Oct 11 1916
GREEN.M.	Moses	1757	Salt Pond Burin	Wm & Mary	Broembeek	22	Oct 9 1917
GROVES.D.	Daniel	1724	Rigolet, Labrador	Fred Malcom & Mary Ann	Monchy-le-Preux	25	Apr 14 1917
GULLAGE.W.F.	William	3260	Catalina	Son of Joseph S	Steenbeek	24	Aug 16 1917
LIEUTENANT							
HOLLOWAY.R.P.	Robert Palfrey		St. John's	Son of Meth. Rev Rob. Edwards & Henrietta	Monchy-le-Preux	30	Apr 14 1917
SERGEANT							
HANNON.F.J.	Frank	2184	Harbour Main	Patrick & Bridget O'Gorman	Broembeek	25	Oct 9 1917
HODDINOTT.L.D.	Ludwig Duncan	2234	St. John's	Augustus & Caroline	Monchy-le-Preux	23	Apr 14 1917
HUSSEY.W.T.	Wm Thomas	356	St. John's	Son of Edward	Monchy-le-Preux		Apr 14 1917
CORPORAL							
HATCHER.H.T.	Henry Thomas	2705	Rose Blanche	George & Amelia	Bailleul	37	Apr 13 1918
LANCE CORPORAL							
HARBIN.W.T.	Wilfred	953	Twillingate	Henry & Elizabeth	Beaumont-Hamel	25	Jul 1 1916
HARDING.H.	Herbert	353	St. John's	Edward & Belinda	Les Fosses Farm/Monchy	23	Apr 23 1917
HOUNSELL.J..M.M.	Japheth	2110	Wesleyville	Henry & Dorcas	Bailleul		Apr 13 1918

LAST NAME AND RANK	FIRST NAME	REG #	PLACE OF ORIGIN	NEXT OF KIN	BATTLE	AGE	DATE OF DEATH
PRIVATE							
HAINES.A.	Albert	1110	Jamestown, BB	John & Rosanna	Beaumont-Hamel	22	Jul 1 1916
HALFYARD.W.	Wallace	3793	Bonne Bay	Wm & Eliza Ann	Keiberg Ridge	19	Oct 3 1918
HALL.J.	James	1935	St. John's	Michael & Mary	Gueudecourt	23	Oct 12 1916
HAMEN.R.J.	Richard Joseph	3037	Creston, Burin	Benjamin & Susie	Ingoyghem	21	Oct 25 1918
HANCOCK.A.	Albert	1853	St. Anthony	Wm & Bessie	Ypres 1918	21	Mar 10 1918
HANN.R.	Robert	3915	Trout River	James & Mary	Bailleul	26	Apr 13 1918
HARDING.E.W.	Ernest William	2949	Little Bay West, Fortune	David & Phoebe	Monchy-le-Preux	21	Apr 14 1917
HARDING.W.	William	995	Renews	Christopher & Mary	Broembeek	29	Oct 9 1917
HARDY.J.	John	760	St. John's	James & Elizabeth	Gallipoli	20	Oct 14 1915
HARRIS.C.V.	Clarence Valentine	3365	Glovertown	Fred. & Mary	Keiberg Ridge	20	Sep 30 1918
HARRIS.G.W.	George William	1321	Humbermouth	Son of John	Beaumont-Hamel	24	Jul 1 1916
HARRIS.H.N.	Harvey Newman	1114	Burgeo	Wm Henry & Evelina	Beaumont-Hamel	20	Jul 1 1916
HARRIS.W.G.	William George	2817	Brooklyn, BB	Job & Sarah	Monchy-le-Preux	17	Apr 11 1917
HART.J.	John	3550	Island Cove, Fogo	Henry & Margaret	Broembeek	25	Oct 9 1917
HART.J.	Jonas	3122	Horwood, Fogo	Martin & Maria	Broembeek	22	Oct 9 1917
HARVEY.H.	Henry	2336	St. John's	Wm & Margaret	Monchy-le-Preux	22	Apr 14 1917
HATFIELD.G.B.	George Bernard	65	St. John's	Stephen & Margaret	Beaumont-Hamel	22	Jul 1 1916
HAYES.P.J.	Patrick Joseph	1239	St. John's	John & Mary	Beaumont-Hamel	19	Jul 1 1916
HEALY.J.J.	John Joseph	2748	St. John's	Son of Michael	Monchy-le-Preux	19	Apr 14 1917
HEANEY.J.P.	James Patrick	476	St. John's	James & Anastasia	Beaumont-Hamel		Jul 1 1916
HEARN.A.	Augustine	1024	St. John's	Wm & Sarah	Monchy-le-Preux	19	Apr 14 1917
HERDER.W.	Wallace	2274	St. John's	H.George & Susannah	Sailly-Saillisel	18	Jan 28 1917
HEWLETT.A.	Armenius	2333	La Scie	Wm & Alfreda	Monchy-le-Preux	21	Apr 14 1917
HICKEY.E.	Edward	1920	Barron Is	Son of Thomas	Marcoing	22	Dec 3 1917
HICKEY.W.	William	1341	St. John's	Cornelius & Johanna	Ypres 1918	26	Mar 10 1918
HISCOCK.A.	Alfred	3447	St. John's	James & Harriet	Ypres 1918	25	Mar 14 1918
HOBBS.C.	Charles	4284	Redcliffe	John Wm & Maria Jane	Ledeghem	25	Oct 20 1918
HODDER.S.	Stewart	2976	Horwood, Fogo	James & Susie	Monchy-le-Preux	32	Apr 14 1917
HOLDEN.L.	Lucas	329	Harbour Main	Wm V. & Alice	Beaumont-Hamel	21	Jul 1 1916

Royal Newfoundland Regiment Tablet Column 6

LAST NAME AND RANK	FIRST NAME	REG #	PLACE OF ORIGIN	NEXT OF KIN	BATTLE	AGE	DATE OF DEATH
HOLLAHAN.J.	Joseph	1133	St. John's	Samuel & Julia	Beaumont-Hamel	26	Jul 1 1916
HOLLETT.G.	George	1799	Port Au Bras, Burin	Wm & Charlotte	Monchy-le-Preux	23	Apr 14 1917
HOLMES.A.	Aubrey	2551	Springdale	Son of Henry	Monchy-le-Preux	22	Apr 14 1917
HOWARD.J.J.	James John	560	St. John's	Capt Patrick & Johanna	Beaumont-Hamel	22	Jul 1 1916
HOYLES.J.	Joseph	2513	Brookfield, BB	Son of Jane	Broembeek	21	Oct 9 1917
HOYLES.O.	Obadiah	3814	Pool's Is, BB	Charles & Mary Jane	Ypres 1918	22	Mar 30 1918
HUSSEY.F.J.	Francis Joseph	1533	Freshwater, St. John's	John & Sarah	Beaumont-Hamel	18	Jul 1 1916
HUSSEY.H.	Harold	2255	St. John's	Wm & Emma	Monchy-le-Preux	21	Apr 14 1917
HUTCHINGS.W.S.	Wiliam	3796	Bonne Bay	Son of Sarah	Bailleul	27	Apr 13 1918
HYNES.W.	Harry	1621	Norris Arm	Esau & Mary	Beaumont-Hamel	21	Jul 1 1916
HYNES.L.	Leonard	5859	St George	Rich. & Margaret	Died at Sea	23	Oct 8 1918
HYNES.L.E.	Lemuel Edward	806	Indian Islands, Fogo	Richard & Maria	Monchy-le-Preux	29	Apr 14 1917
HYNES.W.P.	William Patrick	2726	St. Brendan's	James & Bridget	Monchy-le-Preux	24	Apr 14 1917
Lance Corporal							
IVANY.W.C.	William Cox	1201	Jamestown, BB	Son of Georgina	Monchy-le-Preux		Apr 14 1917
Private							
IVANY.J.A.	John Alfred	3119	Charlton St, St. John's	Martin & Amry	Marcoing	22	Dec 3 1917
IVANY.W.M.	William Mark	3158	English Hr	Jonathan & Sarah	Marcoing	23	Dec 3 1917
2nd Lieutenant							
JUPP.C.H.O.	Clifford Henry Oliver	157	Pulborough, Sussex	Wm & Marion	Beaumont-Hamel	25	Jul 1 1916
JERRETT.F.	Frank	1437	Brigus	Fred & Jane E	Gueudecourt	23	Oct 12 1916
Corporal							
JACKMAN.A.J.	Arthur Joseph	533	St. John's	Francis & Ellen	Monchy-le-Preux	24	Apr 14 1917
Private							
JACKMAN.M.J.	Michael Joseph	733	Bell Island	David J. & Catherine	Beaumont-Hamel	19	Jul 1 1916
JACOBS.F.J.	Frederick James	1297	St. John's	James & Rachel	Bailleul	22	Apr 12 1918
JANES.C.	Charles	3933	Greenspond	Charles & Emma	Ingoyghem	19	Oct 25 1918
JANES.G.	George	3350	Britannia	Henry & Mary	Broembeek	23	Oct 9 1917

LAST NAME AND RANK	FIRST NAME	REG #	PLACE OF ORIGIN	NEXT OF KIN	BATTLE	AGE	DATE OF DEATH
JANES.G.R.	George Robert	1642	Bishop's Falls	James & Harriet	Beaumont-Hamel	29	Jul 1 1916
JOHNSON.A.	Alfred	1571	21 Bitton Ave, Teignmouth	Son of Madeline Rebecca Neiass	Beaumont-Hamel	23	Jul 1 1916
JOHNSON.G.	George	1930	Trouty	James & Emily	Monchy-le-Preux	21	Apr 14 1917
JOHNSON.J.J.	John Joseph	135	St. John's	Andrew & Mary	Beaumont-Hamel	23	Jul 1 1916
SERGEANT							
KEAN.T.J.	Thomas Joseph	2869	St. John's	John & Margaret	Marcoing	21	Dec 3 1917
KELLY.M.F.	Michael Francis	148	37 Cabot St, St. John's	Henry & Elizabeth	Beaumont-Hamel	26	Jul 1 1916
KNIGHT.W.B.	William Blackler	290	355 Southside, St. John's	Frederick W. & Emilie Florence	Beaumont-Hamel	23	Jul 1 1916
CORPORAL							
KING.E.	Ephraim	1572	Catalina	Cephas & Naomi	Bailleul	24	April 12 1918
LANCE CORPORAL							
KENT.M.P.	Martin Patrick	1270	Placentia	James M. & Johanna	Gueudecourt	21	Oct 12 1916
KING.H.A.	Henry	2630	White Point Bonaventure TB	Richard & Phoebe	Bailleul	20	Apr 13 1918
PRIVATE							
KANE.G.	George	208	St. John's	Patrick & Bridget	Marcoing	24	Dec 3 1917
KAVANAGH.E.	Edward	2548	St. John's	John H & Fannie	Monchy-le-Preux	21	Apr 14 1917
KEAN.W.	Wallace	2599	Traytown	Charles & Amelia	Monchy-le-Preux	19	Apr 14 1917
KEARLEY.E.	Eber	1450	Blaketown	Son of Charles	Beaumont-Hamel		Jul 1 1916
KEARSEY.F.	Francis	3265	St. John's	James & Annie	Masnieres	34	Nov 20 1917
KEATING.P.	Patrick	3329	Torbay	Thomas & Mary	Marcoing	20	Dec 3 1917
KEATS.W.	William	203	St. John's	Richard & Elizabeth	Monchy-le-Preux	24	Apr 14 1917
KEEFE.A.	Aloysius	1971	Placentia	Son of Patrick	Monchy-le-Preux	26	Apr 14 1917
KEEPIN.M.	Mack	3299	Fortune	Benjamin & Mary	Masnieres	20	Nov 20 1917
KEEPING.J.G.	James	2917	Lally Cove, Fortune Bay	Edward & Elizabeth	Monchy-le-Preux	29	Apr 14 1917
KEEPING.S.	Stanley	2697	Sydney, NS	James & Agnes	Les Beoufs/Somme	17	Nov 19 1916
KELLY.D.	Daniel	2297	Gambo	Patrick & Agnes	Les Beoufs/Somme	23	Nov 21 1916
KELLY.T.J.	Thomas Joseph	178	Jerseyside	James & Mary Ann	Beaumont-Hamel	26	Jul 1 1916

ROYAL NEWFOUNDLAND REGIMENT TABLET COLUMN 7

LAST NAME AND RANK	FIRST NAME	REG #	PLACE OF ORIGIN	NEXT OF KIN	BATTLE	AGE	DATE OF DEATH
KENDELL.E.W.	Edward William	3110	Ramea Is	Son of Wm Robert	Broembeek	18	Oct 9 1917
KENNEDY.M.F.	Michael Francis	255	St. John's	Nicholas & Margaret	Beaumont-Hamel	22	Jul 1 1916
KING.A.	Aaron	2646	Bonaventure	Noah & Jessie	Marcoing	21	Dec 3 1917
KING.A.	Arthur	2764	Broad Cove, CBN	Silas & Ellen	Monchy-le-Preux	30	Apr 14 1917
KING.J.A.	Joseph Andrew	1356	Broad Cove, CBN	Silas & Dinah	Beaumont-Hamel	22	Jul 1 1916
KING.J.W.	Jabez William	2718	Lewisporte	Matthew & Phoebe	Died at Sea	25	Aug 9 1916
KING.W.J.	William John	2430	Bonaventure	Noah & Jessie	Monchy-le-Preux	24	Apr 14 1917
KNOWLING.W.A.	William	1693	South Branch, St. George	George & Georgina De Villeneuve	Monchy-le-Preux	21	Apr 14 1917
CAPTAIN							
LEDINGHAM.J.A.	James Allan		St. John's	John & Anna Maria	Broembeek	29	Oct 9 1917
CORPORAL							
LUSCOMBE.H.G.	Herbert	1978		Son of Andrew	Gueudecourt	21	Oct 12 1916
LYNCH.T.	Thomas	1355	St. John's	Thomas & Mary Ann	Marcoing	32	Dec 3 1917
LANCE CORPORAL							
LEARY.C.	Charles	1284	St. Ann's, PB	John & Margaret	Broembeek	22	Oct 9 1917
PRIVATE							
LAMBERT.J.	John	3026	St. John's	Richard & Elizabeth	Steenbeek	18	Aug 16 1917
LANE.M.	Malcolm	3192	Fair Island, BB	Grandson of Eli	Bailleul	23	Apr 12 1918
LANNON.M.F.	Michael Francis	967	South East Placentia	James & Esther	Beaumont-Hamel	23	Jul 1 1916
LAWRENCE.W.G.	William	1717	Garnish	Wm & Rebecca	Ypres 1917	25	Sep 28 1917
LE DREW.J.F.	John	2988	Change Is	John G. & Mary	Ypres 1917	29	Jul 10 1917
LEE.A..M.M.	Albert	3216	Riverhead, St. Mary's Bay	John & Mary	Ledeghem	31	Oct 14 1918
LEONARD.J.	James	2865	British Hr	Thomas & Ellen	Monchy-le-Preux	26	Apr 14 1917
LEONARD.M.	Michael	3164	St. John's	Son of Michael	Bailleul	23	Apr 12 1918
LE PAGE.M.	Manuel	3179	Ship Cove Bay, St. George	Son of Claude	Marcoing	19	Dec 3 1917
LE RICHE.J.H.	James	2462	Channel	Son of John	Sailly-Saillisel	18	Jan 28 1917
LE SHANA.W.E.	William Edward	799	Vancouver, BC	Wm & Mabel/Wife Jeannette	Beaumont-Hamel	24	Jul 1 1916
LEUDY.J.	Joseph	1331	Little River, Codroy	Philip & Elizabeth	Gueudecourt	23	Oct 12 1916
LEWIS.J.T.	John	2746	Chapel's Cove	Thomas & Margaret	Bailleul	19	Apr 12 1918
LILLY.W.J.	William John	1034	Hr Grace	James & Agnes	Broembeek	21	Oct 9 1917

LAST NAME AND RANK	FIRST NAME	REG #	PLACE OF ORIGIN	NEXT OF KIN	BATTLE	AGE	DATE OF DEATH
LINFIELD.R.	Roland	2543	Loon Bay	Son of Alfred	Masnieres	23	Nov 20 1917
LITTLE.J.H.	James Hampton	2964	Bonavista	Samuel & Emily	Broembeek	24	Oct 9 1917
LUFFMAN.H.G.	Henry George	2236	Bell Is	Henry & Sarah	Ypres1917	22	Sep 26 1917
LUKINS.J.	John	547	St. John's	Fred. & Johanna/Wife Mary Campbell	Trench Raid	29	Jun 28 1916
LYONS.A.	Allan	1222	Avondale	James & Margaret	Beaumont-Hamel	24	Jul 1 1916
Coy. Sgt. Major							
MILES.V.W.	Victor William	214	St. John's	Henry & Selina	Beaumont-Hamel	31	Jul 1 1916
Corporal							
MANUEL.A..M.M.	Alfred	721	Northern Arm, Botwood	Philip & Alice	Monchy-le-Preux	25	Apr 14 1917
MC GRATH.R.B.	Ronald	2712	Hr Grace	Th. Jos & Alice	Ypres1917	22	Sep 28 1917
MILLER.B.	Benjamin	300	Champney's West	Deborah & Robert	Broembeek	21	Oct 9 1917
Lance Corporal							
MACLEOD.N.C.	Neil Charles	841	St. John's	John Norman & Carrie Martin	Gueudecourt	20	Oct 12 1916
MOORES S.J.	Samuel	943	Freshwater, Bay De Verde	Joseph Jeffers & Mary Charlotte	Gueudecourt	26	Oct 12 1916
Private							
MAC KAY.W.H.	Walter	4105	Channel	Herbert H & Mary E	Keiberg Ridge	18	Oct 2 1918
MADORE.G.A.	George Albert	1458	Wood's Is, Bay of Islands	Alfred & Irene	Monchy-le-Preux	23	Apr 14 1917
MAHER.J.J.	James John	951	Quidi Vidi Rd, St. John's	Wm & Clara	Beaumont-Hamel	20	Jul 1 1916
MANSFIELD.M.	Michael	3590	Kitchuses	Patrick & Mary A	Bailleul	21	Apr 13 1918
MARKS.L.	Levi	2961	Sandy Point, Burin	Charles & Sarah	Monchy-le-Preux	21	Apr 14 1917
MARSH.W.L.	William	2083	Deer Hr	Ezra & Caroline	Gueudecourt	19	Oct 12 1916
MARTIN.J.J.	James	2352	8 Sebastion Street, St. John's	James & Mary	Bailleul	18	Apr 13 1918
MARTIN.R.B.	Richard	2936	Bull Cove, Burin	Frank & Bessie	Monchy-le-Preux	19	Apr 14 1917
MARTIN.S.	Stephen	1998	Kitchens Hill, Hr Grace	Eli & Mary Ann	Marcoing	22	Dec 3 1917
MARTRET.J.	Joseph	1599	254 Gower Street, St. John's	Augustus & Mary Ellen	Beaumont-Hamel	20	Jul 1 1916
MC CARTHY.C.	Charles	5741	Riverhead, Hr Grace	Justin & Mary	Died At Sea	24	Oct 8 1918
MC DONALD.M.P.	Michael	1746	Portugal Cove Rd, St. John's	Patrick & Frances	Bailleul	20	Apr 12 1918

ROYAL NEWFOUNDLAND REGIMENT TABLET COLUMN 8

LAST NAME AND RANK	FIRST NAME	REG #	PLACE OF ORIGIN	NEXT OF KIN	BATTLE	AGE	DATE OF DEATH
MC GRATH.J.	Joseph	3760	Branch	Patrick & Elizabeth	Bailleul	20	Apr 13 1918
MC GRATH.T.W..M.M.	Thomas White	856	St. John's	TJ & Annie	Gueudecourt	20	Oct 11 1916
MC NIVEN.W.R.	William Robert	279	Portugal Cove Rd, St. John's	Fred. & Rosann	Beaumont-Hamel	21	Jul 1 1916
MEADUS.R.	Robert	1013	St. John's	Henry & Susanna	Beaumont-Hamel	20	Jul 1 1916
MEANEY.J.A.	John	2396	St. John's	John T & Mary A	Broembeek	19	Oct 9 1917
MEEHAN.B.	Bernard	1760	St. Mary's	Son of Martin	Gueudecourt	20	Oct 12 1916
MELEE.T.	Thomas	1877	St. John's	Thomas & Sarah	Beaumont-Hamel	19	Jul 1 1916
MERCER.A.	Allan	994	Bay Roberts	Samuel & Susanna	Monchy-le-Preux	20	Apr 14 1917
MERCER.M.J.	Maxwell James	1446	Bay Roberts	Isaac & Anastasia	Beaumont-Hamel	19	Jul 1 1916
MERCER.R.	Robert	1928	Blaketown	Son of Eliel	Beaumont-Hamel	25	Jul 1 1916
MERCER.W.	William	2615	Hr Grace	Leander & Priscilla	Monchy-le-Preux	24	Apr 14 1917
MESHER.C.A.	Charles	1727	Rigolet, Labrador	Ambrose & Mary Ann	Monchy-le-Preux	23	Apr 14 1917
MILLER.G.	George	587	Montreal, QC	Bertha Summerton & William James	Beaumont-Hamel	26	Jul 1 1916
MILLER.W.P.	William Patrick	107	Sydney, NS (Clarenville)	Patrick and Frances J	Buried at Sea Gallipoli	38	Oct 17 1915
MITCHELMORE.G.	George	2872	Flower's Cove	George & Mary Martha	Les Fosses Farm/Monchy	24	Apr 23 1917
MITCHELMORE.I.	Isaac	1810	Flower's Cove	Austin & Elizabeth	Gueudecourt	24	Oct 12 1916
MOONEY.J.R.	James Raymond	920	Placentia	Alfred & Agnes	Beaumont-Hamel	23	Jul 1 1916
MOORES.J.	John	3250	Blackhead, CB	Son of Arthur	Keiberg Ridge	20	Oct 5 1918
MORGAN.W.	William	865	St. John's	John A & Sarah	Beaumont-Hamel	16	Jul 1 1916
MORRIS.E.A.	Edward	1894	St. John's	Isaac C & Fanny	Marcoing	22	Dec 3 1917
MORRIS.K.	Kenneth	412	Lower Island Cove	Joseph & Jane	Beaumont-Hamel	27	Jul 1 1916
MORRIS.W.	William	1581	Robison's Head, St. George	Son of Henry	Gueudecourt	21	Oct 13 1916
MORRISSEY.J.T.	John Thomas	1074	St. John's	Lawrence & Catherine	Beaumont-Hamel		Jul 1 1916
MORTON.J.	Joseph	1791	Burin North	Son of George	Beaumont-Hamel	25	Jul 1 1916
MOSHER.G.	George	4168	Fortune	Saul & Susanna	Ingoyghem	17	Oct 25 1918
MOSS.D.	Daniel	2657	Boston, MA (Gambo)	Thomas & Johanna	Bailleul	22	Apr 12 1918
MOULTON.H.	Herbert	2899	Burin	Thomas Isaac & Eliza	Monchy-le-Preux	21	Apr 14 1917
MOULTON.J.	John	3936	Loon's Cove, Burin	Thomas Isaac & Eliza	Bailleul	19	Apr 13 1918
MOYES.A.	Allan	546	Topsail	Son of Anna Maria	Beaumont-Hamel		Jul 1 1916
MUDFORD.B.	Bennett	2521	Cottle's Is, Twillingate	Mark & Phoebe	Monchy-le-Preux	25	Apr 14 1917
MUGFORD.L.	Luke	2036	Port Albert, Twillingate	John & Mary	Gueudecourt	22	Oct 12 1916

LAST NAME AND RANK	FIRST NAME	REG #	PLACE OF ORIGIN	NEXT OF KIN	BATTLE	AGE	DATE OF DEATH
MULLINGS.G.A.	Gordon	1698	St. John's	Son of Joseph R	Somme 1917	20	Jan 20 1917
MURPHY.E.J.	Edward Joseph	112	Pleasant St, St. John's	Matthew & Mary F	Beaumont-Hamel	24	Jul 1 1916
MURPHY.J.	Joachim	696	Mundy Pond Rd, St. John's	Joseph & Ellen	Buried at Sea, Gallipoli	19	Nov 7 1915
MURPHY.M.	Martin	3655	Duffs, Holyrood	Edward & Martha	Marcoing	24	Dec 3 1917
MURRAY.A.	Archibald	2733	Adams Cove	Edward & Elizabeth	Monchy-le-Preux	23	Apr 14 1917
LIEUTENANT							
NORRIS.S.C	Stephen Casimir	921	St. John's	James & Mary	Gueudecourt	23	Oct 11 1916
CORPORAL							
NEVILLE.R.J..M.M.	Richard	1080	St. John's	Richard & Ellen	Monchy-le-Preux	24	Apr 14 1917
NEWELL.K.S.	Kenneth	1682	Dock, Bareneed	John & Susan	Monchy-le-Preux	23	Apr 14 1917
PRIVATE							
NELSON.C.J.	Charles Joseph	1592	24 Lime St, St. John's	Charles & Bridget	Beaumont-Hamel	24	Jul 1 1916
NEVILLE.W.J.	William John	376	39 Young St, St. John's	Michael & Alice	Monchy-le-Preux	20	Apr 14 1917
NEWHOOK.G.F.	George Frederick	1391	Dildo	John & Lizzie	Beaumont-Hamel	22	Jul 1 1916
NEWMAN.J.	James	2901	Petite Forte	Son of John	Ypres 1918	25	Jan 27 1918
NICHOLS.C.W.	Campbell Withycombe	810	Deer Lake	John HA & M. Elizabeth	Beamont-Hamel	20	Jul 1 1916
NORMAN.W.H.	William	2046	Bay Roberts	Henry & Ellen	Les Fosses Farm/Monchy	23	Apr 23 1917
NORMORE.L.	Levi	2425	Pilley's Island	John & Dinah	Monchy-le-Preux	27	Apr 14 1917
NOSEWORTHY.H.	Herman	354	160 Casey St, St. John's	John & Julia Emma	Beaumont-Hamel	21	Jul 1 1916
NURSE.W.	William	3674	Champneys	Wm & Grace	Bailleul	20	Apr 12 1918
SERGEANT							
OLLERHEAD.W.	William	746	Heart's Content	James & Susannah	Beaumont-Hamel	25	Jul 1 1916
CORPORAL							
O'ROURKE.J.	John	1975	Birch Hill, Bay Roberts	Thomas & Mary	Monchy-le-Preux	24	Apr 14 1917
PRIVATE							
O'BRIEN.J.J.	James John	1378	Topsail	Richard & Mary	Monchy-le-Preux	20	Apr 14 1917

Royal Newfoundland Regiment Tablet Column 9

LAST NAME AND RANK	FIRST NAME	REG #	PLACE OF ORIGIN	NEXT OF KIN	BATTLE	AGE	DATE OF DEATH
O'FLYNN.M.J.	Michael Joseph	727	Grand Falls	David A & Annie	Beaumont-Hamel	22	Jul 1 1916
O'KEEFE.T.J.	Thomas Joseph	923	Ferryland	John & Esther	Sailly-Saillisel	24	Jan 28 1917
O'KEEFE.W.J.	William Joseph	521	St. John's	Peter & Mary	Beaumont-Hamel	21	Jul 1 1916
OLDFORD.H.	Hubert	3183	Hollett's Cove, BB	Andrew & Hananh	Masnieres	26	Nov 20 1917
O'LEARY.J.J.	James Joseph	391	St. John's	Philip & Catherine	Beaumont-Hamel	37	Jul 1 1916
O'NEILL.J.	John	2493	St. John's	Rodger & Kathleen	Monchy-le-Preux	22	Apr 14 1917
O'NEILL.M.J.	Michael Joseph	763	Mount Cashel, St. John's	Brother of A. O' Neill	Beaumont-Hamel	18	Jul 1 1916
O'NEILL.P..M.M.	Patrick	2263	Fermeuse	Michael & Elizabeth	Broembeek	42	Oct 9 1917
O'REILLY.W.	William	2118	Placentia	William & Maggie	Marcoing	22	Dec 3 1917
Coy. Sgt. Major							
PENNY.A.J.	Arthur Joseph	6	English Hr	Arthur & Tryphena	Monchy-le-Preux	25	Apr 14 1917
PORTER.R.B.	Robert Branfitt	896	Grand Falls	John & Mary	Beaumont-Hamel	29	Jul 1 1916
Sergeant							
PETITE.P.	Philip	2059	English Hr West	Jeremiah & Bessie	Monchy-le-Preux	21	Apr 14 1917
PITCHER.W..M.M.	Walter	2115	Old Bonaventure	Archibald & Fanny	Masnieres	28	Nov 20 1917
PITT.P.W.	Percy William	3511	Norbury, Surry, England	Joseph & Anna	Marcoing	22	Dec 3 1917
Corporal							
PITMAN.R.	Richard	400	Lamaline	Robert & Phyllis	Beaumont-Hamel	28	Jul 1 1916
Private							
PALFREY.P.	Patrick	2582	St. John's	John & Margaret	Monchy-le-Preux	18	Apr 14 1917
PARSONS.A.L.	Aubrey	1664	Lumsden North	John & Martha	Beaumont-Hamel	19	Jul 1 1916
PARSONS.B.C.	Bertram	1840	Flat Islands, PB	Walter & Sarah	Gueudecourt	24	Oct 12 1916
PARSONS.C.A.	Charles Albert	1471	Stephenville Crossing	Son of Matilda	Beaumont-Hamel		Jul 1 1916
PARSONS.C.H.	Charles	1708	Sandy Point, St. George	James S & Mary	Gueudecourt	21	Oct 12 1916
PATEY.W.W.	William	1857	St Anthony's Bight, Twillingate	Joseph & Sarah	Monchy-le-Preux	35	Apr 14 1917
PAYNE.N.	Naaman	3429	Parson's Pond	Simon & Julia	Bailleul	20	Apr 13 1918
PEARCE.H.	Hector	1394	Clarenville South	Edmund & Wliza	Monchy-le-Preux	20	Apr 14 1917
PEARCE.S.R.	Samuel	2835	North Side, Twillingate	Andrew Jos & Ophelia	Monchy-le-Preux	23	Apr 14 1917
PELLEY.C.	Clarence	2484	Georges Brook	John & Susan	Arras/Monchy	23	Apr 21 1917
PENNELL.C.	Charles	1428	Curling	Son of Joseph	Monchy-le-Preux		Apr 14 1917

LAST NAME AND RANK	FIRST NAME	REG #	PLACE OF ORIGIN	NEXT OF KIN	BATTLE	AGE	DATE OF DEATH
PENNEY.A.	Alexander William	2696	St. John's	William & Margaret	Monchy-le-Preux	20	Apr 14 1917
PENNEY.J.H.	Josiah	665	Carbonear	Josiah & Anna	Beaumont-Hamel	26	Jul 1 1916
PENNY.W.H.	William	941	Carbonear	Israel & Susannah	Monchy-le-Preux		Apr 14 1917
PENTON.I.	Ignatius	2589	Heart's Desire	Richard & Julia	Monchy-le-Preux	21	Apr 14 1917
PERRY.W.	Warrick	2218	Kelligrews	Charles & Julia	Broembeek	21	Oct 10 1917
PHELAN.W.A.	William	2001	St. John's	James & Mary	Gueudecourt	18	Oct 11 1916
PHILLIPS.G. M.M.& RUSSIAN ORDER OF ST.GEORGE 3RD CLASS	George	1164	Whitbourne	Wm & Sarah	Gueudecourt	27	Oct 12 1916
PIERCEY.B.	Berkeley	421	Hopeall	Isaac & Ida Jane	Monchy-le-Preux	27	Apr 14 1917
PIKE.J.J.	James Joseph	1220	Avondale	Joseph & Winifred	Beaumont-Hamel	19	Jul 1 1916
PIKE.M.E.	Manuel Edward	2666	220 Theatre Hill, St. John's	Lewis & Minnie	Monchy-le-Preux	18	Apr 14 1917
PINSENT.S.	Stewart	1158	Dildo	Samuel & Emma	Beaumont-Hamel	28	Jul 1 1916
PITCHER.C.	Charles	2319	Burgoyne's Cove	Son of Cornelius	Monchy-le-Preux	20	Apr 14 1917
PITCHER.C.	Corbett	1961	New Harbour	Japheth & Eliza	Marcoing	30	Dec 1 1917
PITTMAN.A.H.	Arthur Henry	3404	Pilley's Is	Charles & Mary	Marcoing	24	Dec 3 1917
POLLARD.W.	William	3823	Harbour Deep	Wm & Virtue Ann	Bailleul	18	Apr 13 1918
POWELL.G.	Garland	2816	Happy Adventure	James & Rosanna	Sailly-Saillisel	19	Mar 2 1917
POWER.F.	Francis	2652	St. John's	Michael & Catherine	Monchy-le-Preux	18	Apr 14 1917
POWER.P.	Patrick	2424	Dunville	John & Mary	Bailleul	22	Apr 12 1918
POWER.W.J.	William Joseph	965	St. John's	Michael & Margaret	Les Fosses Farm/Monchy		Apr 23 1917
PRETTY.J.	John	2276	Chapel Arm	Edmund & Sarah	Monchy-le-Preux	19	Apr 14 1917
CAPTAIN							
ROWSELL.R.S..M.C.	Reginald		Bonavista	John & Lydia	Monchy-le-Preux	27	Apr 14 1917
2ND LIEUTENANT							
REID.R.B.	Robert Bruce	593	Bartra, Circular Rd, St. John's	Sir Wm Duff & Lady Reid	Beaumont-Hamel	21	Jul 1 1916
RYALL.W.T.	William Thomas	53	St. John's	Robert & Elizabeth	Beaumont-Hamel	28	Jul 1 1916

Royal Newfoundland Regiment Tablet Column 10

LAST NAME AND RANK	FIRST NAME	REG #	PLACE OF ORIGIN	NEXT OF KIN	BATTLE	AGE	DATE OF DEATH
SERGEANT							
ROMAINE.H.	Harold	2169	Port au Port	John Ernest & Mary Ann	Bailleul	26	Apr 12 1918
ROWE.H.M.	Henry Mott	611	Cathedral Clergy House, St. John's	Wm & Elizabeth	Masnieres	23	Nov 20 1917
CORPORAL							
RYAN.W.J.	William Joseph	133	Southside West, St. John's	William & Catherine	Beaumont-Hamel	25	Jul 1 1916
LANCE CORPORAL							
RIDOUT.G.	Garland	1595	Newtown, BB	Son of Jane	Monchy-le-Preux	21	Apr 14 1917
ROBERTS.F.	Frank	2522	Wild Bight, Green Bay	Hugh & Lydia	Ypres 1918	21	Mar 14 1918
ROLLS.W.	Walter	1494	Bonavista	Samuel & Mary Jane	Broembeek	29	Oct 9 1917
ROWSELL.E.C.	Edward Clayton	571	St. John's	Uriah & Sarah	Beaumont-Hamel	24	Jul 1 1916
PRIVATE							
RANDELL.P.	Peter	1276	Southside, Twilligate	Brother of Bessie	Broembeek		Oct 9 1917
RAYNES.F.	Frederick	1514	St. John's	Robert & Priscilla	Gueudecourt	20	Oct 12 1916
READER.A.	Alexander	1135	Bonavista	Wm S. & Jessie	Sailly-Saillisel	23	Feb 25 1917
REID.J.H.	Joseph	2414	Heart's Delight	Wm & Mary	Monchy-le-Preux	21	Apr 14 1917
REILLY.P.	Peter	2902	Corbin Burin	Son of Patrick	Monchy-le-Preux	21	Apr 14 1917
RENDELL.E.J.	Ernest John	1906	New Harbour	Frederic & Naomi	Gueudecourt	19	Oct 12 1916
RICE.J.J.	John Joseph	1062	St. John's	Patrick & Agnes	Beaumont-Hamel	27	Jul 1 1916
RICHARDS.D.	David	1082	Little Brehat	Jesse & Julia	Monchy-le-Preux	26	Apr 14 1917
RICHARDSON OF.P.	Patrick	1234	St. John's	John & Jane	Beaumont-Hamel	21	Jul 1 1916
RICKETTS.G.	George	1703	Middle Arm, White Bay	Son of John	Marcoing	20	Dec 3 1917
RICKS.S.	Simon	4070	Sop's Arm	Son of George	Keiberg Ridge	21	Sep 29 1918
RIDEOUT.F.	Ford	3736	Cottle's Is, Moreton's Hr	Samuel & Maria	Bailleul	29	Apr 12 1918
RIDEOUT.T.	Thomas	2455	King's Point	Isaac & Eliza	Monchy-le-Preux	21	Apr 14 1917
RIDOUT.S.	Sydney	1258	Cottle's Is, Moreton's Hr	Ambrose & Elizabeth	Beaumont-Hamel	21	Jul 1 1916
RING.T.J.	Thomas	2364	St. John's	Martin & Hannah	Monchy-le-Preux	19	Apr 14 1917
ROBERTS.C.	Cecil	3908	Hermitage	Frederick & Susanna	Ledeghem	18	Oct 14 1918
ROBERTS.J.	John	4042	Burlington	Wm & Jane	Keiberg Ridge	18	Sep 30 1918
ROBERTS.T.S.	Thomas Stephen	3875	Epworth, Burin	Thomas & Mary	Ingoyghem	17	Oct 25 1918

LAST NAME AND RANK	FIRST NAME	REG #	PLACE OF ORIGIN	NEXT OF KIN	BATTLE	AGE	DATE OF DEATH
RODGERS.E.J.	Edward Joseph	355	St. John's	Stephen & Catherine	Beaumont-Hamel	19	Jul 1 1916
RONAN.T.	Thomas	2041	St. John's	Son of Elizabeth	Gueudecourt	33	Oct 12 1916
ROSE.C.	Cecil	3532	Great Hr, Burgeo	Son of Emily	Marcoing	24	Dec 3 1917
ROSE.G.	George	2919	Burgeo	Matthew & Susie	Monchy-le-Preux	19	Apr 14 1917
ROSE.J.	John	2175	Cape St. Francis	Son of Ambrose	Les Fosses Farm/ Monchy	19	Apr 23 1917
ROSE.P.	Peter	2474	Twillingate	Nephew of Peter Clarke	Monchy-le-Preux	20	Apr 14 1917
ROSSITER.M.	Matthew	1538	Fermeuse	Joseph & Ellen	Beaumont-Hamel	20	Jul 1 1916
ROWSELL.G.	Gordon	1466	Exploits, NDB	Son of Emma	Monchy-le-Preux		Apr 14 1917
RUSSELL.J.	John	4358	Bay Roberts	John & Annie	Ledeghem	16	Oct 20 1918
RUSSELL.J.	Joseph	2299	Lewisporte	Wm & Amelia	Somme 1916	21	Oct 18 1916
RUSSELL.M.R.	Melville	2365	Dartmouth, NS	Edward & Mary	Masnieres	18	Nov 20 1917
RYALL.R.S.	Robert	1891	St. John's	Robert & Elizabeth	Gueudecourt	20	Oct 12 1916
2nd Lieutenant							
SMITH.S.R.	Samuel	932	Hr Breton	Son of John	Monchy-le-Preux	27	Apr 14 1917
STEPHENS.J.S.	John Sydney	32	England & St. John's	Son of James	Monchy-le-Preux		Apr 14 1917
Coy. Q.M. Major							
SELLARS.H.	Henry	1414	Harbour Grace	Th & Fannie	Ledeghem	26	Oct 14 1918
Sergeant							
SIMMONDS.W.T.	William Thomas	349	St. John's	James & Jessie/Husband of Lily	Ledeghem	26	Oct 14 1918
Lance Corporal							
SHAVE.E.L.	Edwin	1699	Fogo	Constable Wm Henry & Isobel	Beaumont-Hamel	19	Jul 1 1916
SHIWAK.J.	John	1735	Rigolet	John & Sarah	Masnieres	28	Nov 20 1917
SNOW.F.E..M.M.	Frederick	685	St. John's	George & Dinah	Beaumont-Hamel	21	Jul 1 1916
SNOW.H.F.	Hardy Frederick	322	St. John's	Wm & Naomi	Gueudecourt	21	Oct 12 1916
SPURRELL.F.J.	Frank	979	St. John's	Son of John	Beaumont-Hamel		Jul 1 1916
STARKS.E.G.	Edward	2559	King's Point	Hezekiah & Emma F	Broembeek	20	Oct 9 1917
STRONG.N.W.	Norman Wheatley	1522	Little Bay Is	James M & Lydia	Beaumont-Hamel	20	Jul 1 1916
Private							
SAMSON.N.	Neville	3544	Flat Islands, BB	Edward & Martha Jane	Marcoing	18	Dec 3 1917

Royal Newfoundland Regiment Tablet Column 11

LAST NAME AND RANK	FIRST NAME	REG #	PLACE OF ORIGIN	NEXT OF KIN	BATTLE	AGE	DATE OF DEATH
SARGENT.J.	John	1540	Badger	Michael & Cecilia	Gueudecourt	19	Oct 12 1916
SAUNDERS.E.	Eli	3367	Point Leamington	Adam & Mary	Bailleul	20	Apr 13 1918
SAUNDERS.F.J.	Fred	1913	Griquet	George & Maud	Gueudecourt	21	Oct 12 1916
SAUNDERS.J.	John	3577	Glovertown	James & Sarah	Marcoing	26	Dec 3 1917
SCANLON.D.	David	2088	Boston, MA	Daniel & Elizabeth	Sailly-Saillisel	19	Mar 3 1917
SEALEY.F.	Frederick	3257	Brigus	Sister of Ella Stanley	Broembeek	20	Oct 9 1917
SELLARS.R.A.	Richard Alexander	1728	Western Bay	Son of Mrs Jeremiah Dalton	Somme 1916/Flers	20	Oct 16 1916
SENIOR.R.	Ralph	2880	Flat Islands	Wm Henry & Jane Eliza	Ingoyhem	22	Oct 25 1918
SEWARD.H.	Horatius	172	Clarenville	Adam & Mary Ann	Steenbeek		Aug 16 1917
SHORT.J.	James	1086	Bonavista	Joseph & Bertha	Broembeek	25	Oct 9 1917
SHORT.R.M.	Richard	1202	New Bonaventure	Wm Miller & Annie	Beaumont-Hamel	20	Oct 9 1917
SIMMS.F.F.H.	Frank	2959	Kimberly Farm, Burin	Frank H & Rose C	Marcoing	18	Dec 3 1917
SIMMS.H.	Henry	4045	Pilley's Is	Th & Harriet	Ingoyhem	21	Oct 25 1918
SIMMS.L.	Leaten	1243	St. Anthony	Adam & Mary Ann	Broembeek	22	Oct 9 1917
SIMMS.R.R.	Robert Ronald	576	St. Anthony	Adam & Mary Ann	Beaumont-Hamel	19	Jul 1 1916
SIMPSON.R.G.	Ronald Gordon	3373	St. John's	Robert & Sophie	Bailleul	19	Apr 12 1918
SINNOTT.S.	Sylvester	2089	St. John's	Michael & Sarah	Monchy-le-Preux	23	Apr 14 1917
SLATTERY.P.J.	Patrick	2983	St. John's	James & Julia	Ypres 1918	20	Mar 13 1918
SMITH.W.H.	William	2868	Swift Current	Robert & Elizabeth	Monchy-le-Preux	21	Apr 14 1917
SMITH.Z.	Zachariah	1467	Snook's Hr	John Peddle & Mary Ann	Beaumont-Hamel	23	Jul 1 1916
SNELGROVE.J.C.	John Charles	895	St. John's	Samuel & Annie	Beaumont-Hamel	24	Jul 1 1916
SNOW.J.	Joseph	1870	Griquet	Stephen & Amanda	Keiberg Ridge	26	Sep 29 1918
SOMERTON.F.C.	Frederick Charles	1342	Trinity	Frederick & Caroline	Buried at Sea, Gallipoli	27	Nov 25 1915
SOPER.M.	Morley	1259	Port Aux Basques	Th & Elizabeth	Buried at Sea, Gallipoli	26	Dec 29 1915
SOUTHCOTT.T.	Thomas	3852	Grand Falls	Arthur & Laura Eugenie	Bailleul	20	Apr 12 1918
SPARKES.G.J.	George Joseph	253	Bell Is	George & Annie	Beaumont-Hamel	19	Jul 1 1916
SPENCER.H.B.	Bennett	2592	Back Hr, Twillingate	Mark & Mary Jane	Les Fosses Farm/Monchy	23	Apr 23 1917
SPENCER.H.M.	Herbert Maxwell	3640	Springdale	George & Mary Jane	Bailleul	18	Apr 12 1918
SQUIRES.C.A.	Cecel	3353	Gambo	Joseph & Lydia	Broembeek	21	Oct 9 1917
SQUIRES.J.	John	2343	Southside, St Johns	Benjamin & Emily Sarah	Bailleul	20	Apr 12 1918
STOCKLEY.F.	Frederick	3518	Wesleyville	Son of Wm	Ypres 1918	20	Mar 11 1918
STOCKLEY.L.	Levi	3726	Oakwood Ave, Toronto	Th & Helen Wells/ Husb of Agnes	Bailleul	30	Apr 13 1918

LAST NAME AND RANK	FIRST NAME	REG #	PLACE OF ORIGIN	NEXT OF KIN	BATTLE	AGE	DATE OF DEATH
STONE.H.	Henry	2099	Bonaventure	Levi & Sarah	Monchy-le-Preux	29	Apr 14 1917
STRATHIE.H.G.	Harry Groves	494	Bonavista	Ronald & Mary	Beaumont-Hamel	23	Jul 1 1916
STRATTON.F.	Frederick	2715	Valleyfield	Abel & Elizabeth	Monchy-le-Preux	32	Apr 14 1917
STUCKLESS.A.	Adolphus	3839	Comfort Cove	Emma & Samuel	Bailleul	21	Apr 13 1918
2nd Lieutenant							
TAYLOR.G.H.	George Hayward	28	St. John's	Eugene F & Mary	Beaumont-Hamel	24	Jul 1 1916
Corporal							
THOMAS.F.G.	Frederick Gordon	1784	St. John's	Frederick & Tryphena	Monchy-le-Preux	20	Apr 14 1917
Lance Corporal							
TAYLOR.E.F.	Eugene Fred	2525	St. John's	Eugene F & Mary	Monchy-le-Preux	21	Apr 14 1917
TILLEY.H.	Henry	307	St. John's	Wm James & Selina	Monchy-le-Preux	26	Apr 14 1917
TUCKER.W.	Walter	880	St. John's	Stephen & Lucy	Buried at Sea Gallipoli	21	Oct 25 1915
Private							
TARRANT.E.	Elias	2446	Burnt Arm, Botwood	John W & Julia	Monchy-le-Preux	23	Apr 14 1917
TAYLOR.A.P.	Alfred Penny	897	St. John's	G. Hedley & Dorcas Guy	Beaumont-Hamel	22	Jul 1 1916
TAYLOR.G.	George	2080	St. John's	Son of George	Les Fosses Farm/Monchy	25	Apr 23 1917
TAYLOR.H.	Hedley	1129	St. John's	David & Susanna	Steenbeek	23	Aug 16 1917
TAYLOR.R.H.	Richard Hall	1973	St. John's	Eugene F & Mary	Monchy-le Preux	23	Apr 14 1917
TEIXEISA.J.	Joseph	3424	Oporto, Portugal	Brother of Ignez	Ypres 1918	19	Mar 13 1918
TILLY.L.	Lawrence	1404	Clarenville	Walter & Annie	Broembeek	21	Oct 9 1917
TIZZARD.G.	Gordon	753	The Battery, St. John's	Simeon & Elizabeth	Bailleul	22	Apr 10 1918
TRASK.H..M.M.	Heber	3156	Elliston	Thomas & Alice	Ingoyghem	21	Oct 25 1918
TUCKERJ.	Joshua	2684	Winterton	John & Anna	Buried at Sea Gallipoli	20	Apr 14 1917
TUFF.F.P.	Frank Paine	1694	St. John's	Edmund & Serena	Gueudecourt	18	Oct 12 1916
TUFF.J.	Jabez	2606	Templeton, BB	Wm & Selina	Les Beoufs/Somme	26	Nov 19 1916

ROYAL NEWFOUNDLAND REGIMENT TABLET COLUMN 12

LAST NAME AND RANK	FIRST NAME	REG #	PLACE OF ORIGIN	NEXT OF KIN	BATTLE	AGE	DATE OF DEATH
TULK.R.	Ralph	4207	Ladle Cove	Gabriel & Mary Ann	Ledeghem	19	Oct 14 1918
TWYNE.A.J.	Abram James	3259	Bear Cove, White Bay	James & Susan	Ypres 1918	22	Mar 28 1918
UPWARD.P.	Pearce	2777	Harry's Hr, Green Bay	Brother of Arthur & Blanche	Broembeek	20	Oct 9 1917
CORPORAL							
VOKEY.P.	Philip	2240	Dildo	Philip & Mary Ann	Broembeek	24	Oct 9 1917
PRIVATE							
VAUGHAN.J.	Joseph Patrick	800	St. John's	Henry & Ellen	Monchy-le-Preux	20	Apr 14 1917
VISCOUNT.J.F.	John Francis	1065	Dunville	John & M.R.	Buried at Sea, Gallipoli	20	Oct 30 1915
VOISEY.L.M.	Leo Michael	959	St. John's	Son of Richard	Broembeek	21	Oct 9 1917
VOISEY.R.P.	Richard Patrick	1462	St. John's	Son of Richard	Monchy-le-Preux	29	Apr 14 1917
VOKEY.H.	Herbert	2614	Little Hr, Twilligate	Philip Henry & Emily Ann	Monchy-le-Preux	19	Apr 14 1917
SERGEANT							
WATERFIELD.J.R..M.M	Joseph Ross	789	St. John's	Joseph & Jessie/Wife Annie	Broembeek	22	Oct 9 1917
WINSOR.E.	Edgar	472	Wesleyvilles	John & Mary	Broembeek	23	Oct 9 1917
CORPORAL							
WHITE.A.C.	Albert Clarence	1374	Catalina	Wm John & Virtue	Monchy-le-Preux	19	Apr 14 1917
WILLS.H.	Herbert	2185	Grand Falls	Frederick Wm & Mary	Somme 1916	18	Dec 8 1916
LANCE CORPORAL							
WELLS.J.W.	Joseph Warren	1147	St. John's		Steenbeek		Aug 14 1917
WESTCOTT.H.T.	Harry	1805	Carbonear	Henry & Margaret	Beaumont-Hamel	23	Jul 1 1916
WHITE.H.	Hollie	3847	Cottell's Cove, New Bay	William	Bailleul	21	Apr 12 1918
WINTER.R.M.	Randolph Milligan	908	Burin North	John & Adelaide	Beaumont-Hamel	29	Jul 1 1916
PRIVATE							
WADE.E.	Edgar	1917	Elliston	Maria	Marcoing	22	Dec 3 1017
WAGG.A.F.	Albert	3270	Stepaside, Burin	Stephen & Selina	Marcoing	19	Dec 3 1917
WALSH.M.F.	Michael Francis	399	Placentia	Patrick & Catherine	Beaumont-Hamel	25	Jul 1 1916
WALTERS.G.	Gilbert	620	Champney's East	John & Mary	Gueudecourt	30	Oct 12 1916
WATKINS.R.J.	Robert james	1426	Botwood	Ephraim & Jane	Beaumont-Hamel	26	Jul 1 1916

LAST NAME AND RANK	FIRST NAME	REG #	PLACE OF ORIGIN	NEXT OF KIN	BATTLE	AGE	DATE OF DEATH
WATTS.J.P.	James Pittman	397	French's Lane, St. John's	Charles Wesley & Elizabeth	Gueudecourt	25	Oct 12 1916
WAY.N.	Norman	2883	Bonavista	Arthur & Mary Jane	Monchy-le-Preux	22	Apr 14 1917
WEBBER.H.	Hubert	2693	Harbour Grace	George & Caroline	Bailleul	23	Apr 14 1918
WELLS.C.	Clarence	2681	Montreal, QC	Matthew & Phoebe	Monchy-le-Preux	19	Apr 14 1917
WELLS.H.A.	Harry Augustus	3943	Bay Roberts	Robert James & Ruth	Ingoyghem	24	Oct 25 1918
WELLS.R.	Robert	4107	St. John's	Wm J. & Mary Jane	Keiberg	28	Sep 29 1918
WEST.E.	Edward	1588	Apsey Cove, Fogo	Rose Shelley	Beaumont-Hamel	21	Jun 28 1916
WEST.S.	Stanley	1460	Halifax, NS	Joseph & Sarah	Beaumont-Hamel	23	Jul 1 1916
WHITE.F.	Frederick	1481	Durrell's Arm	Edward & Sarah	Beaumont-Hamel	24	Jul 1 1916
WHITE.F.J.	Frederick	3542	Princeton, BB	Robert & Elizabeth	Marcoing	24	Dec 3 1917
WHITE.R.	Richard	2354	Bacon Cove	Nicholas & Bridget	Arras/Les Fosses Farm	21	Apr 21 1917
WHITE.W.	Willis	739	Comfort Cove	CS & Sarah	Beaumont-Hamel	20	Jul 1 1916
WHITE.W.A.	William Arthur	1632	Rattling Brook	Son of John	Beaumont-Hamel	21	Jul 1 1916
WIGHT.A.	Arthur	944	Shoal Brook, Bonne Bay	Samuel & Annie	Beaumont-Hamel	26	Jun 28 1916
WILLIAMS.A.	Alexander	2051	Springdale	Martin & Lucy	Gueudecourt	26	Oct 12 1916
WILLIAMS.H.	Hugh	3581	Springdale	Martin & Lucy	Marcoing	19	Dec 1 1917
WILLIAMS.J.	James	3881	Baine Hr	John & Olivia	Ledeghem	21	Oct 14 1918
WILLIAMS.R.V.	Raymond Victor	2847	Heart's Content	Adam & Lydia	Broembeek	20	Oct 9 1917
WINSOR.G.	George	1845	Wesleyville	David & Annie	Beaumont-Hamel	18	Jul 1 1916
WISEMAN.A.	Adolphus	2050	Little Bay Islands	Job & Jane	Gueudecourt	21	Oct 12 1916
WISEMAN.M.S.	Marcus Stanley	3332	Heart's Delight	James & Leonora	Marcoing	20	Dec 3 1917
WOODFORD.P.J.	Patrick	1965	Twillingate	Alfred & Elizabeth	Gueudecourt	27	Oct 12 1916
WOODMAN.K.B.	Kenneth Berkley	1627	New Harbour	Edward & Susanna	Beaumont-Hamel	22	Jul 1 1916
WOOLRIDGE.J.R.	James Robert	1993	Trinity	John & Phoebe	Monchy-le-Preux	18	Apr 14 1917
SERGEANT							
YOUNG.J.B.	John Bertram	816	St. John's	Robert & Helen	Sailly-Saillisel	20	Feb 25 1917
PRIVATE							
YETMAN.M.	Michael	3359	St. John's	Son of of Andrew/ Wife Amelia	Steenbeek	40	Aug 16 1917
YOUNG.H.L	Henry Leslie	2113	Greenspond	Alex & Ellen	Gueudecourt	21	Oct 12 1916

Royal Naval Reserve Tablet Column 1

LAST NAME	FIRST NAME	NAVAL #	NEXT OF KIN	PLACE OF ORIGIN	AGE	DATE OF DEATH	VESSEL
LEADING SEAMAN							
BLUNDON.A.	Allan	1496x	Brother of Herbert	Gloucester, MA	21	Aug 24 1917	SS HEATHERSIDE
COATES.H.	Harold	2130x	Philip & Emma Coates	Fogo	29	Apr 28 1917	SS HERMES
DYKE.J.W.	John Walter	1215x	Wm & Elizabeth	Salvage Bay	26	Feb 7 1917	SS NINIAN (PRESIDENT III) COLLIER 737
MILLER.G.H.	George	1727x	Son of Jane Janes	Spaniard's Cove, TB	21	Dec 16 1917	SS HALIFAX
O'KEEFE.E.	Edward	1266x	John & Alice	St. John's	28	Aug 11 1917	SS LYNORTA
SOMERTON H.	Herbert	720x	Mathew & Maria	Portugal Cove	27	Apr 20 1917	SS PORTLOE
WELLS.D.	Daniel	833x	David & Mary Jane	Wild Cove, Seal Cove, WB	29	Mar 17 1918	HM MINE SWEEPER SEAGULL
SEAMAN							
ANDERSON.J.	James	1558x	Prosper & Mary A	Mouse Island, Channel	22	Jan 14 1916	HMS EBRO
AYLES.A.	Alexander	1697x	James & Mary	Bonavista	28	Jan 25 1917	HMS LAURENTIC
BABSTOCK.W.T.	William Thomas	477x	Lemual Joseph & Eliza	Happy Adventure	32	Apr 30 1917	HM TRAWLER ARFRON
BARNES.E.	Enos	1220x	Mathew & Elizabeth	Port Union	33	Jan 13 1915	HMS VIKNOR
BARBOUR.G.	George	1681x	Robert & Martha	Port Rexton	24	Nov 10 1918	HM TRAWLER RENARRO
BENNETT.L.J.	Leonard Joseph	1331x	Wm & Agnes		29	Dec 21 1915	HM MINE SWEEPER LADY ISMAY
BENOIT.J.J.	James John	2272x	John & Alice	Stephenville	24	Jan 25 1917	HMS LAURENTIC
BERRIGAN.J.T.	John Thomas	1455x	Edward & Elizabeth	Renews	32	Jan 18 1918	HM TRAWLER GAMBRI
BRACE. A.	Albert	1219x	Richard & Mary	Chance Cove, TB	20	Jan 13 1915	HMS VIKNOR
BRENTON.G.	George	1502x	George & Ellen	Port Au Bras	23	Jan 25 1917	HMS LAURENTIC
BRINSTON. L.	Leslie	305x	Rb.Wm & Amelia/ Wife Susie	North Hr, PB	32	Jan 25 1917	HMS LAURENTIC
BROWN. E.	Edmond	815x	Husband of Mary	Fogo	29	Mar 11 1915	HMS BAYANO
BRYAN.E.	Edward	1284x	John & Elizabeth Tucker	St. John's	25	Feb 3 1915	HMS CLAN MCNAUGHTON
BUTLER. P.	Peter	2174x	Wm & Anne	Harbour Grace	22	Feb 3 1915	HMS CLAN MCNAUGHTON
CHAFE.J. Served as AVERY.J.	Jack	1825x	Albert & Eliza		22	May 4 1917	SS TRANSYLVANIA
CHAFE.W.H.	William Henry	1283x	Henry & Hannah	Forest Pond, Goulds	21	Feb 3 1915	HMS CLAN MCNAUGHTON
COADY.T.F.	Timothy Francis	1293x	Son of Anna	St. John's	30	Feb 3 1915	HMS CLAN MCNAUGHTON
COATES.G.	George	1147x	Philip & Emma	Fogo	29	Jan 13 1915	HMS VIKNOR
COPLEY.T.	Thomas	1162x	Son of Jane Ann Snow & George Copley	Salmon Cove, CBN	24	Mar 11 1915	HMS BAYANO

LAST NAME	FIRST NAME	NAVAL #	NEXT OF KIN	PLACE OF ORIGIN	AGE	DATE OF DEATH	VESSEL
CROCKER.S	Stanley	2178x	John Charles & Jane	Heart's Delight	19	Feb 3 1915	HMS CLAN MCNAUGHTON
CUMBY.E.	Ersatus	1777x	George & Hannah		24	Jan 25 1917	HMS LAURENTIC
DAWE.W.H.	William Henry	1174x	Son of Rebecca	Ship Cove, Port de Grave	21	Feb 29 1916	HMS ALCANTARA
DELANEY.T.S	Timothy Samuel	2080x	Joseph & Lucy	St. George	22	Aug 25 1917	SS SYCAMORE
DICKER.S.	Stephen	1240x	George & Jane	Flat Island	22	Feb 3 1915	HMS CLAN MCNAUGHTON
DYER.W.G.	William Gerard	2170x	Son of Helen	Logy Bay	31	Feb 3 1915	HMS CLAN MCNAUGHTON
DYKE.G.	Gilbert	702x	John Martin & Luisa	Salvage Bay	23	Jan 13 1915	HMS VIKNOR
FAREWELL.J.	Joseph	927x	Son of Margaret	Seal Cove, Fogo	30	Mar 11 1915	HMS BAYANO
FOWLOW.J.	John	688x	Abram & Mary/wife Lillian	Goose Cove, Trinity	32	Feb 7 1919	H.M. PADDLE MINESWEEPER ERIN'S ISLE
FREAKE.E.	Ephraim	2213x	Son of Mary	Joe Batt's Arm	21	Jan 25 1917	HMS LAURENTIC
FREAKE.W.	William	2210x	Aaron & Sarah A.	Joe Batt's Arm	19	Jul 20 1917	H.M. PADDLE MINESWEEPER QUEEN OF THE NORTH
GOSS.E.	Eldred	357x	Husb of Elizabeth	Queen's Cove, Random South TB	30	Jan 25 1917	HMS LAURENTIC
GOSSE.W.	Walter	1400x	Peter & Elizabeth	Tilton CB	23	Aug 23 1915	HM TRAWLER
GREENE.B.	Barton	873x	Wm & Lucina		24	Mar 11 1915	HMS BAYANO
GREENING.J.	James	411x	Joseph & Jane	Summerville, BB	28	Jan 13 1915	HMS VIKNOR
HALL.R.H.	Richard Hugh	1733x	Alexander & Elizabeth	Cambell's Creek, Bay St. George	25	Jul 24 1918	MH TRAWLER LOCHIEL
HALLET.A.	Albert	931x	Jones & Sarah	Flat Island, BB	23	Feb 3 1915	HMS CLAN MCNAUGHTON
HENNESSEY.P.J.	Patrick Joseph	2245x	Patrick Jos. & Mary		18	Sep 19 1917	SS ST RONALD
HISCOCK.J.	John	1764x	Wm & Amelia	Hillview, Random Island	20	May 31 1916	HMS INVINCIBLE
HULAN.E.M.	Edward	1645x	George F & Rosanna	Middle Barachoix Bay, St. George	23	May 22 1917	HM TRAWLER MERSE
HURLEY.T.	Thomas	1233x	Son of Joseph	Island Hr, Fogo	25	Aug 18 1916	HMS MACEDONIA
HYNES.J.W.	James	1533x	Charles & Dinah	Port au Port	19	Oct 12 1915	HM ARMED DRIFTER OLIVAE
JACKSON.T.	Thomas	2180x	Son of Alice	Brigus	21	Jan 13 1915	HMS VIKNOR
JAMES.J.	John	1869x	Wm & Mary	Forteau, Labrador	26	Mar 7 1917	HM TRAWLER VIVANTI
JERRETT.L.	Levi	1218x	Wm & Mary	Boyd's Lane, St. John's	23	Jan 13 1915	HMS VIKNOR
JONES.W.	William	1678x	John & Jane	Trinity East	24	Dec 9 1915	HM TRAWLER RETURNO
KAVANAGH.T.J.	Thomas Joseph	2171x	James & Katherine	Logy Bay	18	Feb 3 1915	HMS CLAN MCNAUGHTON
KEHOE.W.J.	William	2173x	Michael Thomas & Christina	Riverhead, Hr Grace	26	Feb 3 1915	HMS CLAN MCNAUGHTON
KELLY.A.	Albert	874x	John & Emmeline	Cupids	24	Jan 13 1915	HMS VIKNOR
KING.W.	William	2181x	Nephew of Thomas Hayes	Brigus	20	Mar 11 1915	HMS BAYANO

ROYAL NAVAL RESERVE TABLET COLUMN 2

LAST NAME	FIRST NAME	NAVAL #	NEXT OF KIN	PLACE OF ORIGIN	AGE	DATE OF DEATH	VESSEL
KNIGHT. T.	Thomas	1297x	Wm & Annie	St. John's	31	Feb 3 1915	HMS CLAN MCNAUGHTON
LE DREW. G.H.	George Hussey	1531x	James John & Eliza		19	Oct 12 1915	HM ARMED DRIFTER OLIVAE
LEWIS. P.	Philip	1213x	Son of Melina Reynolds & Frederick	Caplin Cove, Bay De Verde	20	Jan 13 1915	HMS VIKNOR
MAHER.L.J	Leo Joseph	2277x	Son of Ellen		19	Jun 12 1917	HM TRAWLER CAREW CASTLE
MARTIN.A.	Alexander	1224x	Son of Rebecca	St. John's East	23	Jan 13 1915	HMS VIKNOR
MARTIN.S.	Sylvester	915x	Thomas & Mary	St. John's	24	Mar 11 1915	HMS BAYANO
MILLER.H.	Harold	1578x	John & Jane	La Scie	19	Dec 30 1915	SS CLAN MACFARLANE
MORGAN.F.	Frederick	1209x	Son of Joseph	Portugal Cove	19	Jan 13 1915	HMS VIKNOR
MORGAN.J.T.	John Thomas	1255x	Son of Joseph	Seal Cove, CBS	18	Feb 3 1915	HMS CLAN MCNAUGHTON
MORGAN.W.G.	William	1190x	George Henry & Sarah	Seal Cove, CBS	17	Jan 13 1915	HMS VIKNOR
MORRIS.W.	Walter	1282x	Son of Amelia	Blow-Me-Down, Port de Grave	19	Feb 3 1915	HMS CLAN MCNAUGHTON
MUGFORD.J.	Jacob	531x	Wm & Lavinia/wife Ethel May/Sister Susan	St. John's	31	Jan 25 1917	HMS LAURENTIC
MUGFORD.N.	Nathan	1171x	Nathaniel & Elizabeth Ann	Leopold Post Office, Quebec	24	Feb 29 1916	HMS ALCANTARA
MURPHY.L.	Lawrence	1817x	James & Sarah	Port de Grave	22	Jan 25 1917	HMS LAURENTIC
MURRAY.J.	James	1446x	John & Margaret	Conception Harbour	21	Jan 25 1917	HMS LAURENTIC
O'BRIEN.P.J.	Patrick	2172x	Richard J & Matilda		19	Feb 3 1915	HMS CLAN MCNAUGHTON
OSMOND.G.A.	Gerald Augustus	1287x	Husband of Mary		26	Feb 3 1915	HMS CLAN MCNAUGHTON
PARSON S.J.	John	932x	John & Mary A	St. John's	23	Jan 13 1915	HMS VIKNOR
PEACH.H.W.	Henry	901x	Wm Henry& Elizabeth/ Wife Elsie May	Shearstown	25	Jan 13 1915	HMS VIKNOR
PEACH.W.H.	William	1001x	Charles & Margaret	Arnold's Cove	21	Mar 11 1915	HMS BAYANO
PEDDLE.A.	Alec	389x	David & Mary Ann/ Wife Julia	Red Hr, PB	29	May 28 1918	HMS DIRK
PHILLIPS.R.	Robert	1441x	Son of Wm	40 LeMarchant Rd, St. John's	29	Apr 20 1917	XHM TRAWLER OTHONNA
PIERCEY.C.A.	Charlie	1000x	Benjamin & Martha (Peach)	Burgoynes Cove, TB	21	Mar 11 1915	HMS BAYANO
PIKE.F.	Francis	2175x	Son of Susan	Red Hr, PB	21	Feb 3 1915	HMS CLAN MCNAUGHTON
POWER.J.J.	John Joseph	2275x	Son of Alice	Water Street, Hr Grace	18	Mar 29 1917	HMS Q 20
PRINCE.H.H.	Harold Heber	1973x	Son of Lizzie	St. John's	21	Jan 18 1918	HM TRAWLER GAMBRI
PUDDICOMBE.W.	William	2136x	Frederick & Annie	Charleston, BB	28	Jan 25 1917	HMS LAURENTIC

LAST NAME	FIRST NAME	NAVAL #	NEXT OF KIN	PLACE OF ORIGIN	AGE	DATE OF DEATH	VESSEL
RALPH.C.	Charles	706x	Stephen & Leah	Flat Is, BB	24	Jan 13 1915	HMS VIKNOR
RANDALL.F.	Frederick	816x	John & Elizabeth	Fogo	26	Jan 25 1917	HMS LAURENTIC
RANDALL.R.	Ralph	2176x	John & Elizabeth	Elliot's Cove, Random Is	20	Feb 3 1915	HMS CLAN MCNAUGHTON
ROGERS.S.	Simeon	1138x	Willis & Sarah/Wife Bertha	St. John's	32	Jan 25 1917	HMS LAURENTIC
ROSE.J.	James	1444x	James & Dorcas	Victoria, Carbonear	24	Feb 12 1917	HM TRAWLER EUSTON
ROWE.C.	Charles	1122x	John & Ann	Trinity	21	Jan 13 1915	HMS VIKNOR
ST CROIX.W.	William	1222x	Joseph & Esther	Trepassey	22	Jan 13 1915	HMS VIKNOR
SIMMONS.E.F.	Eugene	1285x	LH & Anne	Spruce Brook	20	Feb 3 1915	HMS CLAN MCNAUGHTON
SMART.E.	Edward	1227x	Samuel & Fanny	Saunders Cove, Alexander Bay	19	Jan 13 1915	HMS VIKNOR
SMITH.L.	Luke	979x	Husb of Isabella	Butler Cove, Random South, TB	30	Jan 25 1917	HMS LAURENTIC
SNOW.R.J.	Randell Joseph	1256x	Son of Elizabeth	Mundy Pond Rd, St. John's	20	Feb 3 1915	HMS CLAN MCNAUGHTON
SPARKES.E.	Eli	862x	Isaac & Mary J.	Shearstown	24	Jan 13 1915	HMS VIKNOR
SPARKES.SAML.	Samuel	2047x	Ebenezer & Susan (Janes)	St. John's	19	Dec 8 1916	HMM TRAWLER DAGON
SPARKES.STPHN.	Stephen	1538x	Rueben & Fanny	Georgetown, Brigus	22	Oct 12 1915	HM ARMED DRIFTER OLIVAE
SPURRELL.W.J.	Walter	969x	John & Diana/wife Lizzie A	Trouty, TB	21	Apr 8 1917	SS TORRINGTON
SQUIRES.R.J.	Richard	1280x	Richard J & Elizabeth	St. John's	21	Feb 3 1915	HMS CLAN MCNAUGHTON
STANLEY.H.A.	Harold	2184x	Charles & Maude	Kilbride/Goulds	20	Mar 11 1915	HMS BAYANO
STEED.D.	Dugald	1032x	Jos Geo. & Annie M.	Little Catalina	22	Oct 28 1916	HM TRAWLER BRADFORD
STONE.E.	Edward	1295x	Edward & Isadora	Bell Island	22	Feb 3 1915	HMS CLAN MCNAUGHTON
STRICKLAND.W.	Walter	789x	John & Fanny/ wife Emily C	Frenchman's Cove, Bay of Islands	27	Dec 20 1917	SS WARSAW
STRINGER.G.	George	1259x	Wm T & Mary Ann	Little Heart's Ease	21	Jan 13 1915	HMS VIKNOR
TUCKER J.C.	John Charles	895x	John Geo. & Sarah Fanny/wife Mary Ann	Ship Cove, Port de Grave	31	Jan 25 1917	HMS LAURENTIC
WALSH. D.	Douglas	1214x	Son of Mary Ann Hutchings	Cow Head	20	Jan 13 1915	HMS VIKNOR
WARREN A.J.	Albert James	2179x	Eli & Mary A	Glovertown	22	Jan 13 1915	HMS VIKNOR
WATKINS.J	Joseph	2177x	Henry & Ellen	Summerford, NDB	23	Feb 3 1915	HMS CLAN MCNAUGHTON
WHALEN. S.	Simeon	1156x	Wm & Alfreda	Caplin Cove, Random TB	24	Mar 11 1915	HMS BAYANO
WOOLDRIDGE.W.M	William Mark	1490x	Charles & Elizabeth	Fogo	22	Oct 12 1915	HM ARMED DRIFTER OLIVAE
YETMAN. C.	Clement	1458x	Moses & Selina	Hr Grace South	25	Jan 25 1917	HMS LAURENTIC
YOUDEN. G.	George	611x	Henry & Jessie	Bull Cove	25	Jan 13 1915	HMS VIKNOR
YOUDEN. T.	Thomas	670x	Henry & Jessie	Bull Cove	26	Jan 13 1915	HMS VIKNOR
YOUNG W	Wallace	1884x	Son of Ellen	Flat Bay, St. George	21	Jan 25 1917	HMS LAURENTIC

Endnotes

See Bibliography for complete references.

Note: *The Newfoundland War Diary* (*The 1st Battalion Royal Newfoundland Regiment War Diary*) was a diary kept by a high-ranking battalion officer to record the movements and actions of the Newfoundland Regiment while on active service. It opens in September 1915, when the Regiment embarked at Gallipoli, and did not close until the end of the war. The collections of pages are grouped roughly by month. Often there is an appendix attached that contains information such as battlefield casualties, letters in praise of the Regiment, drafts, and descriptions of the battles. The originals are kept in Great Britain, but there is a transcribed copy in the Sydney Frost Collection in the Provincial Archives of Newfoundland and Labrador (PANL).

[1] General De Lisle, Commander of the 29th Division, in a letter to Newfoundland Governor Davidson describing the battle of Beaumont-Hamel. G.W.L. Nicholson, p. 281.

[2] *The Daily News*, June 10, 1918.

[3] Marine Court of Enquiry into the Loss of the Steamship Beverly, GN 124, PANL; also *The Daily News*, 1918.

[4] Ibid.

[5] Ibid.

[6] When the "First Five Hundred" reached England they were placed under the command of a Canadian officer. Rumours abounded that the Regiment would be amalgamated with an under-strength Canadian Unit. The men took particular umbrage at the fact that they were mistaken by the British as Canadians and certainly did not want the unit to disappear within the Canadian contingent. G.W.L. Nicholson, p. 123.

[7] These words by Mustafa Kemal Ataturk were enshrined in a monument to his enemies on the Gallipoli Peninsula in 1934. Mustafa Kemal was in command of the Turkish 19th Division at the time of the Allied invasion of Gallipoli in April 1915. He was a superb military strategist and the successful defence of Gallipoli is largely due to his bravery and the high esteem his troops held for him. After the war he led the Turkish people in a series of campaigns to oust occupying forces. By 1923 he established the modern secular state of Turkey with himself as President. The name Ataturk (Father of the Turks) was bestowed upon him by the Turkish Parliament. Today there are monuments erected in Australia and New Zealand, reciprocating the respect he gave to his former enemies at Gallipoli. Source: Australian War Memorial: http://www.anzacday.org.au/education/tff/rememwords.html.

[8] Sydney Frost Collection, MG9, PANL. This citation would have appeared originally in *The London Gazette*.

[9] Letter provided by Bruce King. Miss Buckley was John 'Jack' Lukins' sister-in-law.

[10] *Book of Newfoundland*, V. 1, p. 390.

[11] Ibid, p. 392. Lt. Gen. Sir Aylmer Hunter-Weston commanded the 29th Division during the invasion of Gallipoli and was promoted to Commander of the British VIII Corps before the end of that campaign. He was in command of VIII Corps at the Battle of the Somme; the 29th Division was one of the divisions under his command.

[12] G.W.L. Nicholson, p. 281.

[13] *The Evening Herald*, St. John's, July 29, 1916.

[14] Ibid.

[15] *I Remain your Loving Son*, documentary.

[16] Ibid.

[17] Ibid.

[18] Ibid.

[19] Letter provided by Jack Connors. Many of the missing men at Beaumont-Hamel were thought to be prisoners of war for quite a few months. Whether the Newfoundland Government delayed the news to soften the blow to the country or whether they actually believed that so many were captured on July 1 is debatable.

[20] Ibid.

[21] G.W.L. Nicholson, p. 314.

[22] Cyril Gardner Service Record, PANL; G.W.L. Nicholson, p. 330. This story of Gardner's single-handed capture of 72 Germans was slated to be published in one of London's major newspapers. However, there are conflicting stories. Lord Cavan (Field-Marshall Frederick Lambart) had written the account while he was in command of the XIII Corps: "The Sergeant Major of that Battalion [Newfoundland] went out on his own initiative with some stretcher bearers in clear daylight to help pick up our wounded ... While doing so he saw a German officer looking over the parapet ... [Gardner] waved to the officer and approached him

carefully." Hadow responded to Lord Cavan's story: "… which is not absolutely true and accurate … and you know how easily stories are exaggerated." Hadow, in response, seemed reluctant to heap too much praise on Gardner's actions, but in the end forwarded the story much as Lord Cavan had written (with some minor adjustments). Another account from the 87th Brigade Commander about the incident: "A small party of the Newfoundland Regt. who were holding the left of the Brigade front, seeing a chance of taking prisoners left their trenches with bombs and succeeded in taking 70 odd prisoners." No one seems to know why Gardner was out there without a gun, and Hadow may have been a little piqued at the way Gardner had spurned authority when bringing the Germans back to their front lines. Hadow himself was nowhere near this action as he was on medical leave in Great Britain and did not return to the Battalion until after the actions at Monchy-le-Preux in April. The account presented here came from Nicholson and is considered to be the most correct version; it is assumed that Nicholson culled the story from interviews with men that were there.

[23] *Newfoundland War Dairy*, April 1917.

[24] Ibid.

[25] Haig's End of Year Dispatch 1917, sourced from Great War Documents Online.

[26] *Newfoundland War Dairy*, April 1917.

[27] Cyril Gardner Service Record, PANL.

[28] *Newfoundland War Dairy*, August 1917.

[29] G.W.L. Nicholson, p. 384.

[30] Sydney Frost Collection, MG9, PANL.

[31] *Newfoundland War Dairy*, August 1917.

[32] H.G. Barrett Service Record, PANL. He is the source of the discrepancy in the count of the number of men listed on the Regimental Tablet. For many years sources cited 591 names on the tablet. His name appears to be excluded from the count because he was also commemorated on the Tyne Cot Memorial to the missing. Especially troubling is the fact that his body was found, identified in 1921, and still does not have a headstone in the Artillery Wood Cemetery. At the very least, a special memorial should be erected in his name there. The quote on this page is from a telegram sent on August 11, 1921, by J.L. Murphy, assistant to Padre Thomas Nangle, Newfoundland's Director of War Graves, Registration & Enquiries to the Newfoundland Department of Militia. Another former Newfoundland Regiment soldier, who left the fold in early 1915 under arguable circumstances and joined a Canadian Regiment, was later missing in action. His name is inscribed on the Menin Gate Memorial in Ypres. Herbert W. Blackall of St. John's may be the only member or former member of the Royal Newfoundland Regiment who went missing during the war and is not commemorated at Beaumont-Hamel. He is listed in *The Newfoundland Book of Remembrance* as are most identified Newfoundlanders who served with Canadian forces.

[33] Patrick O'Neill Service Record, PANL.

[34] Battle of Cambrai: http://en.wikipedia.org/wiki/Battle_of_Cambrai_(1917). From this action the Germans learned a valuable strategy and in World War II they employed the blitzkrieg based upon the British assault on November 20.

[35] R. H. Tait, *Veteran Magazine*, April 1922.

[36] Letter from the Trenches, *The Daily News*, January 12, 1918. Letters from soldiers were a common sight in *The Daily News*. The writers wrote anonymously and were subject to censorship. Frank "Mayo" Lind wrote many letters that were later published in book form after his death at Beaumont-Hamel. He got his nickname from the Mayo cigarettes he pined for in one of his letters. People in St. John's responded by raising money and purchasing the Newfoundland-made cigarettes to supply all the troops.

[37] Ibid.

[38] Letter from the Trenches, *The Daily News*, January 12, 1918.

[39] Benjamin Benoit Service Record, PANL.

[40] Letter from the Trenches, *The Daily News*, January 12, 1918.

[41] Ibid.

[42] G.W.L. Nicholson, p. 422.

[43] Letter from the Trenches, *The Daily News*, January 12, 1918.

[44] Joseph Babstock Notebook. This notebook was given to him while he was a prisoner at Schneidemuhl Gefangenlanger (POW camp). He recorded his capture, his movements while in captivity, and a little about camp life. He spent most of 1918 in the same small NCO (Non-Commissioned Officer) compound as Walter Thistle, a Blue Puttee, who was also captured at Cambrai, but found his way to Schneidemuhl via a different route. The photo of five men in the "Legacy" pages of this book may be a commemorative of the five men who approached the Schneidemuhl Camp Kommandant to complain about working conditions for NCOs, in violation of the Geneva Conventions. They were physically threatened and may have been given the impression they were to be executed when they were loaded onto a train shortly after this incident. Instead, 120 NCOs were moved to a smaller compound in Grosborn where the only work was foraging for food and collecting firewood. Not all was rosy here, as Joe put it: "Worst luck, no Frauliens."

[45] Letter from the Trenches, *The Daily News*, January 12, 1918.

[46] Joseph Babstock Notebook.

[47] From Patrick McGill, *Soldiers' Songs*, 1917. This poem was not written by McGill but was included as a sample of songs sung in the trenches. Also known as "Far, Far From Wipers."

[48] *Newfoundland War Diary*. This may have been the first time the Regiment was made aware of the King's assent to designate the title "Royal" to the Regiment. The actual date of the assent, according to different sources, is either December 1917 or January 1918.

[49] *Newfoundland War Diary*, April, 1918.

[50] Ibid.

[51] Ibid.

[52] Ibid.

[53] Maurice Gregory Connors Service Record, PANL.

[54] This scroll accompanied the Dead Man's Penny that was sent to all families of soldiers who died in the service of the British Empire. Veterans Affairs Canada; Canadian Virtual War Memorial.

[55] Brigadier-General Cayley, Commander of the 29th Division. G.W.L. Nicholson, p. 460.

[56] *Newfoundland War Diary*, October, 1918.

[57] Ibid.

[58] Admiral of the Fleet Sir Roger Keyes. Statement made during a debate in the House of Commons in 1936. Nearly two decades after WWI, the British were still praising the actions of the Newfoundland Royal Naval Reserve: "There is another question in regard to the Naval Reserves that I should like to mention. The Newfoundland Royal Naval Reserve which was composed of fishermen who spend their lives in the cod schooners and sealing in the Arctic. They are splendid, hardy people, the finest small-ship seamen in the world. They did splendid service in the War. Many will remember the armed merchantmen of the Tenth Cruiser Squadron which were engaged in the German blockade and patrolled hundreds of miles from land in Mid-Atlantic. Their duties necessitated boarding suspicious vessels in all sorts of weather. These Newfoundland fishermen to a great extent formed the boats' crews who carried out this arduous and dangerous work. The re-establishment of the Newfoundland Reserve would be of very great benefit to the Service and to Newfoundland which is going through hard times. It is our oldest colony and it breeds a splendid seafaring race. It would not cost very much to re-establish the force. It means only a small drill ship at St. John's and it is well worth considering. If, unhappily, we are ever at war again the seafarers of Great Britain will have to play a great part in defeating the submarine menace. Our fishing population is shrinking, and in this connection I should like to read a few words from a letter from a very distinguished naval officer who spends his leisure trying to help the Lifeboat Service: 'I visit the coasts of Great Britain and Ireland and find that most of the fishermen are oldish men. They are not being replaced by their sons, whose educational advantages lead them to prefer shore occupations. They do not like the long hours at sea and they like to keep dry and warm. Every possible encouragement that we can give to seafarers who can stand wet and cold is all to the good, and I hope my suggestion will be favourably considered by the Admiralty.'" UK Parliament Online: hansard.millbanksystems.com/commons/1936/mar/19/navy-estimates-1936.

[59] Veterans Affairs Canada; Canadian Virtual War Memorial.

[60] Oral history, Maude Pinsent (nee Andrews), Maude Beecham's grand-daughter.

[61] Pearce Upward Service Record, PANL. This statement was made by William Cotton of the 20th Lancaster Fusiliers. He was the Methodist minister for Little Bay Islands and married a local girl. He took great interest in the soldiers from Newfoundland. "His body was found by my men and was buried at the edge of D'Houthulst Forest, Belgium (where the Koekiut Road meets the Forest), Map Reference Hazebrouck 5A Edition 2 1/100,000 L.I. We found him lying on that road with a Lewis Gun still on his shoulder, and it was right there where we buried him." Cotton would return to his flock in Newfoundland after the war.

[62] Jabez King Service Record, PANL. His death may have been the result of meningitis. The official Honour Roll indicates that he was buried at sea from the HMS *Laurentic*. His own service record and the telegram copies state that he died on the SS *Sicilian* on its return voyage to Newfoundland. The vessel is pictured on p. 421, V. 1, *Book of Newfoundland*; somewhere in that mass of soldiers was Jabez William King. The ship carried 300 passengers and 500 Regiment soldiers, according to Mortimer Hawker of Carbonear. Mortimer took ill on July 20, a day after leaving St. John's, but survived. Mortimer succumbed to tuberculosis in April 1918 after having his hand amputated and is buried in Carbonear.

[63] Frederick Charles Somerton Service Record, PANL.

[64] *Evening Herald*, July 29, 1916.

[65] Alex Templeton Collection. Newspaper Article Extract: The Evening Telegram, November 12, 1917. Author Unknown, which is how it was published because of censorship.

[66] Ibid.

[67] Letter from Thomas Nangle to Newfoundland Prime Minister Sir Richard Squires, GN 2, PANL. In commemorating Newfoundland's war dead, Nangle initially wanted to have all the names of dead brought home, and did not want a caribou as a symbol on Newfoundland soil. He felt that the impact would be lessened on

the Newfoundland people, however, the caribou as a symbol of Newfoundland (and the Regiment) would be instantly recognizable in Europe. While countries erected battlefield memorials similar to Newfoundland's National War Memorial on Duckworth Street, Nangle (and Cochius) felt that a truly unique battlefield monument in Europe should be crowned by the Regimental symbol. The caribou monument located in Bowring Park was purchased and donated by Major William Howe Green, a Liverpool-born architect, an officer of the Royal Newfoundland Regiment, and grandson of Benjamin Bowring. This caribou may have been the one that graced the outside of the Newfoundland Pavilion during the British Empire Exhibition at Wembley in 1924-25.

[68] Rudolph Cochius, *The Veteran Magazine*, April 1924.

[69] Ibid.

[70] Ibid.

[71] Ibid.

[72] Ibid.

[73] Westminster Abbey, History of the Unknown Warrior.

[74] John Shiwak letter to friend, source: Veterans Affairs Canada.

[75] John Shiwak Service Record, PANL. Oddly, though it is recorded on a number of occasions, the seven to ten men (accounts differ) who were killed by this lone artillery shell are recorded as having died on the 20th, when in actual fact, the date they died was the 21st. Dr. H.Paddon, the father of Dr. Anthony Paddon, was a Grenfell Mission doctor administering to northern Newfoundland and coastal Labrador. Communications were difficult along the coast during winter and this letter was sent to his sister so she could relay the information to Shiwak's family in the spring.

[76] Sydney Frost Collection, mg9, PANL, and nf.archives.net. Originally published in *The London Gazette*, a copy exists in Frost's service file and also in a file gleaned by Sydney Frost from *The London Gazette* of all the gallantry awards made to the Regiment.

[77] Ibid.

Sources Consulted

BOOKS AND ARTICLES:

Andrews, Gerald. *Heritage of a Newfoundland Outport: The Story of Port de Grave*. St. John's: Jesperson, 1997.
Browne, Gary, and McGrath, Darrin. *Soldier Priest*. St. John's: DRC Publishing, 2006.
Cave, Joy B. *What Became of Corporal Pittman?* Portugal Cove: Breakwater Books Ltd., 1976.
Cave, Nigel. *Beaumont Hamel Newfoundland Park Somme*. Barnsley: Leo Cooper, 2003.
Cave, Nigel, and Horstall, Jack. *Cambrai: The Right Hook*. Barnsley: Leo Cooper, 1999.
Cochius, R. H. K. "Marking the Trail of the Caribou." *Veteran Magazine* 4.1 (April 1924): 16–24.
Facey-Crowther, Dr. (Ed.). *Lt Owen Steele of the Newfoundland Regiment: Diaries and Letters*, Montreal & Kingston: McGill-Queen's University Press, 2002.
Fox, Colin. *Monchy le Preux: Arras*. Barnsley: Leo Cooper, 2000.
Gallishaw, John. *Trenching in Gallipoli*. St. John's: DRC Publishing, 2005 (reprint, originally published during World War I).
Gilbert, Martin. *The Battle of the Somme*. Toronto: McClelland & Stewart, 2006.
Holmes, Richard. *Tommy: The British Soldier on the Western Front 1914-1918*. London: Harper Perennial, 2005.
Horwood, Andrew. *Newfoundland Ships and Men*. St. John's: The Marine Researchers, 1971.
Johnson, J. H. *Stalemate*, London: Rigel, 2004.
Lewis, John E. (Ed.). *Eyewitness World War I*. New York: Carroll & Graf, 2003.
Lind, Frank. *The Letters of Mayo Lind*. St. John's: Creative Publishers, 2001.
MacAllister, Anthony. *Regimental Pilgrimage*, pamphlet, 2006.
MacFarland, David. *The Danger Tree*. Toronto: Vintage Canada, 2000.
McGill, Patrick. *Soldiers' Songs*. London: Herbert Jenkins Ltd., 1917.
Murphy, Leo. "Newfoundland's Part in the Great War," *Book of Newfoundland*, Volume 1. Joseph Smallwood (Ed.). St. John's: Newfoundland Book Publishers, 1937.
Nicholson, G.W.L. *The Fighting Newfoundlander: A History of the Royal Newfoundland Regiment*. Montreal & Kingston: McGill-Queen's University Press, 2006.
Palsingham, Ian. *All the Kaiser's Men*. Shroud: Sutton Publishing, 2003.
Parsons, David. *Pilgrimage*. St. John's: DRC Publishing, 2009.
Parsons, David. *The Best Small Boat Men in the World*. St. John's: DRC Publishing, 2009.

Robertshaw, Andrew, and Kenyon, David. *Digging the Trenches: The Archeology of the Western Front*. Barnsley: Pen and Sword, 2008.
Smallwood, Joseph, et al. (Ed.) *Encyclopedia of Newfoundland*, Volumes 1 – 5. St. John's: Newfoundland Book Publishers (1967) Ltd, 1984.
Stacey, A. J. *Memoirs of a Blue Puttee*. St. John's: DRC Publishers, 2002.
Tait, R.H. "The Royal Newfoundland Regiment at Cambrai." *Veteran Magazine* 2.1 (April 1922): 17-40.
The Times History of the War. Vol. 1 - 22, London: The Times, 1916-1921. [A series beginning in 1916 that is an encyclopedia of WWI.]
White, Jack A. *Streets of St. John's*, Vol. 3. St. John's: Creative Publishers, 1992.
Willmot, H.P. *World War I*. London: Dorling Kindersley, 2003.
Winter, Denis. *Haig's Command*. London: Penguin Books, 2001.

ARCHIVES:

The AC Hunter Library, St. John's, NL:
The Daily News (St. John's, NF) 1914-1933.
The Evening Telegram (St. John's, NF) 1914-1933.
The Evening Herald (St. John's, NF) July 29, 1916.
The Telegram (St. John's, NL) July 2, 2009.
The Veteran Magazine (St. John's, NF) 1920-1924.

The National Archives of Great Britain:
The 1st Battalion Royal Newfoundland Regiment War Diary [commonly know as *The Newfoundland War Diary*].
The National Archives, Documents Online, Great Britain <http://www.nationalarchives.gov.uk/documentsonline/>
The Newfoundland War Diary (*The 1st Battalion Royal Newfoundland Regiment War Diary*) was a diary kept by a high-ranking battalion officer. Put out each month or every second month, the diary was a daily log of the movements and actions of the Newfoundland Regiment while on active service. They entered service in September 1915, and the last monthly publication was in December 1918. The originals are kept in Great Britain. There is a copy in the Sydney Frost Collection in the Provincial Archives of Newfoundland and Labrador.

Provincial Archives of Newfoundland and Labrador, The Rooms, St. John's, NL:
Individual War Service records GN 19.
The Great War Veterans' Association MG 592.
Sydney Frost Collection MG 9.
MG 439.
MG 632.
Office of the Colonial Secretary GN 2.
World War I Records GN 2.14.
Newfoundland Patriotic Association GN 2.14.130.
Patriotic Associations and the Newfoundland Patriotic Fund GN 2.14.270.
Marine Court of Enquiry into the Loss of the Steamship Beverley GN 124.
Robert Holland Tait Fonds MG 26.

Queen Elizabeth II Library, Memorial University of Newfoundland, St. John's, NL:
Thomas Nangle Collection, Archives & Special Collections.

The Royal Newfoundland Regiment Museum, St. John's, NL:
Various displays, documents, maps, scrapbooks and photographs.

DOCUMENTARIES:

I Remain your Loving Son, CBC/Springwater Documentary, 1999.
The Blue Puttees, War Amp Documentary, 1992.

INTERNET SOURCES:

Aboriginals in WWI: Newfoundland and Labrador Heritage: http://www.heritage.nf.ca/law/aboriginals_gw.html
The Australian War Memorial, various brigade diaries: http://www.awm.gov.au/ also http://www.anzacday.org.au/education/tff/rememwords.html
Battle of Cambrai: http://en.wikipedia.org/wiki/Battle_of_Cambrai_(1917)
Canadian Biography Online: www.biographie.ca
CBC.ca:
http://www.cbc.ca/canada/newfoundland-labrador/story/2009/07/02/war-memorial-702.html
Canadian Virtual War Memorial:
http://acc.gc.ca/remembers/sub.cfm?source=collections/virtualmem
First World War.Com: www.firstworldwar.com
The Great War Forum: http://1914-1918.invisionzone.com/forums/
Great War Primary Document Archive: Photos of the Great War: www.gwpda.org/photos
Harper, Ken. Taissumani: A Day in Arctic History: November 20, 1917 – In Memory of John Shiwak, Inuit Sniper, November 17, 2006. http://www.nunatsiaqnews.com/archives/61124/opinionEditorial/columns.html
The Labrador War Memorial: http://www.themdays.com/memorial.html Michael Martin
Maritime Quest: www.maritimequest.com
Netflora.co.uk: www.thebigsky.smugmug/photos/207489740-d.jpg (Forget-me-not)
Newfoundland Grand Banks Genealogy Website: http://ngb.chebucto.org/
Newfoundland Great War Heritage Project: www.nfarchives.net
Trinity Historical Society Archives, Trinity NL. A0C 2S0:
The Battle of the Somme: A generation Lost but Never Forgotten: www.newfoundlandandthesomme.com
World War 1 – A Commemoration of Residents from the Trinity and Area: www.virtualmuseum.ca
Uboat.net: www.uboat.net
UK Parliament Online: www.parliament.uk - hansard.millbanksystems.com/commons/1936/mar/19/navy-estimates-1936
Westminster Abbey: www.westminster-abbey.org

OTHER:

Royal Canadian Legion Br # 32. (portrait)
Joseph and Mary Kate Babstock Collection. Author Possession.

INDIVIDUALS WHO CONTRIBUTED THEIR KNOWLEDGE AND PERSONAL COLLECTIONS OF MEMORABILIA:

Myron Arnold
Catherine Ball
Linda Bell
Dan Breen
Gary Browne
Chris Butt
James Cleary
Jack Connors
Oswyn Dawe
Joe Dobbin
Barney Dooley
Rita Dooley
Frank Galgay
Alan and Ben Gardner
Aubrey Halfyard
John Kennedy
Bruce King
Kay King
Tony McAllister
Ron Penney
Maude Pinsent
Shirley Reid Gardner
Wayne Slaney
Alex Templeton
Avril Williams

VISUAL CREDITS

Every reasonable effort has been made to trace the ownership of material reprinted in this book and to make full acknowledgement for its use. The publisher would be grateful to know of any errors or omissions so they may be rectified in subsequent editions.

2,3,4,5,6: Author's Collection; 7: Alex Brennan; 9: Author's Collection; 10: Author's Collection; 12: Provincial Archives of Newfoundland and Labrador; 13: Author's Collection; 14: (bottom right) Author's Collection, (bottom left) Trinity Historical Society, (top center) Author's Collection, (background) City of St. John's Archives; 15: (bottom center) Veterans Affairs, (top right) Chris Butt, (background) City of St. John's Archives; 16: (background) City of St. John's Archives; 17: Author's Collection; 18: (top left) Provincial Archives of Newfoundland and Labrador, (background) City of St. John's Archives; 19: (top right) Rita Dooley; (bottom right) Author's Collection; (background) Royal Newfoundland Regiment; 20: (top center) Royal Newfoundland Regiment, (left) Alex Templeton, (right) Royal Newfoundland Regiment, (background) Royal Newfoundland Regiment; 21: Provincial Archives of Newfoundland and Labrador, (background) Royal Newfoundland Regiment; 22: (top left) Royal Newfoundland Regiment, (bottom right) Provincial Archives of Newfoundland and Labrador, (background) Royal Newfoundland Regiment; 23: (top right, bottom right) Provincial Archives of Newfoundland and Labrador, (background) Royal Newfoundland Regiment; 24: (top right) Chris Butt, (bottom left) Royal Newfoundland Regiment, (background) Provincial Archives of Newfoundland and Labrador; 25: (background) Author's Collection, (bottom right) Provincial Archives of Newfoundland and Labrador; 26: (bottom center, top left) Veterans Affairs Virtual War Memorial, (background) Royal Newfoundland Regiment; 27: (top right) Veterans Affairs Virtual War Memorial, (background) Royal Newfoundland Regiment, (bottom left) Courtesy of Wikipedia Public Domain, (bottom right, top right) Author's Collection; 28: (top right) Frank Galgay, (top left, center) Dan Breen, (bottom) Bruce King, (right, background) Author's Collection; 29 (background) Provincial Archives of Newfoundland and Labrador; 30: Provincial Archives of Newfoundland and Labrador; 31 (top left, bottom left) Veterans Affairs Virtual War Memorial, (bottom right) Shirley Reid, (background) Royal Newfoundland Regiment; 32: Veterans Affairs Virtual War Memorial, (background) Royal Newfoundland Regiment; 33: (bottom right) Royal Newfoundland Regiment, (left) James F. Cleary, (right) Veterans Affairs Virtual War Memorial, (background) Author's Collection; 34: (bottom left) Author's Collection, (top left) Veterans Affairs Virtual War Memorial, (background) Royal Newfoundland Regiment; 35: (top right, center) Royal Newfoundland Regiment, (bottom right) Veterans Affairs Virtual War Memorial, (background) Royal Newfoundland Regiment; 36: (left) Veterans Affairs Virtual War Memorial, (right) Maude Pinsent, (background) Royal Newfoundland Regiment; 37: (right) Trinity Historical Society, (bottom right) Alan and Ben Gardner, (background) Author's Collection; 38: (left) Newfoundland Regiment Virtual War Memorial, (right) Veterans Affairs Virtual War Memorial, (background) Author's Collection; 39: (bottom right) Rita Dooley, (left center) Royal Canadian Legion Branch #32, Bay Roberts, (right) Veterans Affairs Virtual War Memorial, (background) Royal Newfoundland Regiment; 40: Veterans Affairs Virtual War Memorial, (background) Author's Collection; 41: (top right) Myron Arnold, (bottom right) Trinity Historical Society; 42: (top left) Chris Butt, (bottom right) Caroline Ball, (background) Royal Newfoundland Regiment; 43 (top right) Chris Butt, (far left) Royal Newfoundland Regiment, (second from left) Wayne Dove, (second from right) Royal Newfoundland Regiment, (far right) Veterans Affairs Virtual War Memorial, (center) http://digital--angel.deviantart.com/art/Stock-Old-Paper-52365179, (background) Royal Newfoundland Regiment; 44: N & M Press http://www.ww1battlefields.co.uk/flanders/images/lang/steenbeek.jpg, (background) Royal Newfoundland Regiment; 45: (top right) Veterans Affairs Virtual War Memorial, (background) Royal Newfoundland Regiment; 46: (center) Memorial University of Newfoundland and Labrador Archives, (far bottom right) Wayne Slaney, (top center) Joe Dobbin, (top left, right) Veterans Affairs Virtual War Memorial, (far left) Veterans Affairs Virtual War Memorial, (background) Author's Collection; 47: Veterans Affairs Virtual War Memorial, (bottom) Wikipedia Public Domain, (background) www.gwpda.org/photos; 48: (top, bottom) Veterans Affairs Virtual War Memorial, (background) Tony MacAllister; 49: Caroline Ball, (background) Tony MacAllister; 50 (top left) Veterans Affairs Virtual War Memorial, (background) Author's Collection; 51: (top right) Veterans Affairs Virtual War Memorial, (bottom right, background) Author's Collection; 52: (top left) Wikipedia Public Domain, (bottom left) Veterans Affairs Virtual War Memorial, (background) Author's Collection; 53: Veterans Affairs Virtual War

Memorial, (bottom, background) Author's Collection; 54: Author's Collection; 55: (right) Author's Collection, (background) Wikipedia Public Domain; 56 (top left) www.gwpda.org/photos, (bottom left) Veterans Affairs Virtual War Memorial, (background) Royal Newfoundland Regiment; 57: (top right) Veterans Affairs Virtual War Memorial, (bottom right, botton left) Authors Collection; 58: Veterans Affairs Virtual War Memorial, (background) Author's Collection; 59: Linda Bell, (background) Author's Collection; 60: Royal Newfoundland Regiment, (background) Author's Collection; 61: (top right) Authors Collection, (background) Provincial Archives of Newfoundland and Labrador (PANL B-1722); 62: (top right) Provincial Archives of Newfoundland and Labrador (PANL NA-1529), (top left) Author's Collection, (bottom left) Veterans Affairs Virtual War Memorial; 63: Veterans Affairs Virtual War Memorial, (bottom right) Michael W. Pocock and www.maritimerequest.com; 64:(bottom left) Maude Pinsent, (top left, background) Author's Collection; 65: (top right) Provincial Archives of Newfoundland and Labrador (PANL F 37-17), (center) Maude Pinsent, (bottom left, bottom right) Author's Collection; 66: (bottom left) Royal Newfoundland Regiment, (center) Oswyn Dawe, (top left, top right) Rita Dooley, (background) Author's Collection; 67: (top right, bottom right) Author's Collection, (background) Netflora. UK; 68: (top left) Author's Collection, (bottom right) Memorial University of Newfoundland and Labrador Archives, (background) Netflora. UK; 69: (bottom right) Caroline Ball, (left) Veterans Affairs Virtual War Memorial, (background) Author's Collection; 70: (background) Author's Collection; 71: Author's Collection, (bottom right) Provincial Archives of Newfoundland and Labrador (PANL NA-27-44); 72: (top left) Veterans Affairs Virtual War Memorial, (bottom left) Author's Collection, (bottom right) Provincial Archives of Newfoundland and Labrador (PANL B3-215), (background) Author's Collection; 73: (bottom left) Trinity Historical Society, (top right) Linda Bell, (bottom right) Veterans Affairs Virtual War Memorial, (bottom left, background) Author's Collection; 74: (top left, top center) James Cleary, (far right) Chris Butt, (bottom center) Royal Newfoundland Regiment, (center) Author's Collection; 75: (top right) Chris Butt, (center left) Royal Newfoundland Regiment, (bottom left) Alex Templeton; 76: Alex Templeton; 77: (bottom left) Author's Collection, (bottom right) Thomas Nangle Collection Archives and Special Collections, Queen Elizabeth II Library, MUN, PANL F-15-6, (bottom right) Author's Collection, (background) Author's Collection, (center right) Royal Newfoundland Regiment; 78: (bottom left) Royal Newfoundland Regiment Museum, (top left) Caroline Ball, (background) Royal Newfoundland Regiment; 79: (bottom right, background) Memorial University of Newfoundland and Labrador Archives, (top right) Author's Collection; 80: (top left) Memorial University of Newfoundland and Labrador Archives, (center left, bottom left, background) Royal Newfoundland Regiment; 81: (bottom right) Memorial University of Newfoundland and Labrador Archives, (top right, background) Author's Collection; 82: Caroline Ball, (bottom center) Memorial University of Newfoundland and Labrador Archives, (background) City of St. John's Archives; 83: Author's Collection, (top right) Royal Newfoundland Regiment, (top far right) Royal Newfoundland Regiment, (center right) Wikipedia Public Domain, (background) Author's Collection; 84: Veterans Affairs Virtual War Memorial, (background) Author's Collection; 85: Michael Martin, Labrador, (background) Author's Collection; 86: Veterans Affairs Virtual War Memorial; 87: (left) Trinity Historical Society, (bottom right) Ron Penney, (top right) Rita Dooley; 88: (bottom) Royal Newfoundland Regiment, (top left, background) Author's Collection; 89, 90: Author's Collection; 91: (top right) Caroline Ball, (bottom right) Royal Newfoundland Regiment, (background) Author's Collection; 92: Caroline Ball, (background) Author's Collection; 93 (top right) Alex Templeton, (background) Author's Collection; 94: Author's Collection; 95: (bottom right) Myron Arnold, (background) Author's Collection; 96-98, 100-105: Author's Collection

All background images on Mercantile Marine Tablet Column pages courtesy of the author. All background images on Newfoundland Royal Naval Reserve and Royal Newfoundland Regiment Tablet Column pages courtesy of Provincial Archives of Newfoundland and Labrador.

FRANK GOGOS was born and raised in St. John's, NL. He holds a degree in history and Newfoundland studies. An ardent historical researcher, he has covered such topics as Newfoundland and the Great War, culture, and genealogy, and chases the ghosts of individuals long past.

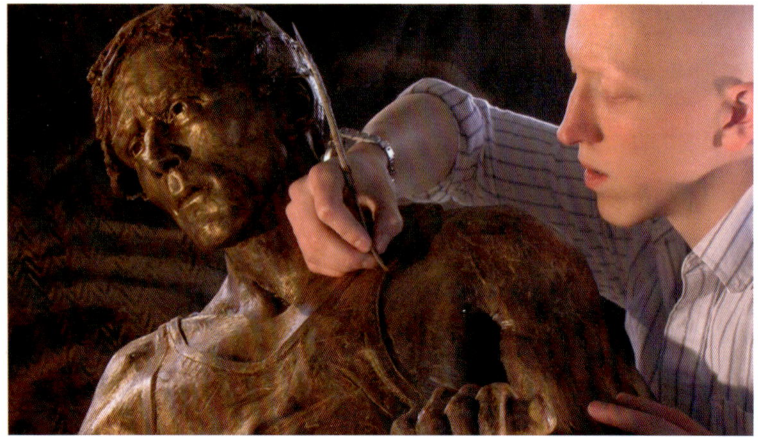

MORGAN MACDONALD is an emerging artist/ bronze sculptor who has created *The Rower* at Quidi Vidi Lake, *A Time* at George Street, and the replica of the Bronze Tablets for Bowring Park (all in St. John's, NL). Born in Corner Brook and transplanted to St. John's, MacDonald attended the Visual Arts Program at Grenfell College, and holds a business degree from Memorial University. His passion for Newfoundland is evident in all his work.

Contact the authors at knownuntogod@hotmail.co.uk